A Maine Summer Island

The Story of Bustins

Also from Islandport Press

Billy Boy by Jean Mary Flahive

Contentment Cove by Miriam Colwell

Young by Miriam Colwell

Stealing History by William D. Andrews

Windswept by Mary Ellen Chase

Mary Peters by Mary Ellen Chase

Silas Crockett by Mary Ellen Chase

My Life in the Maine Woods by Annette Jackson

Shoutin' into the Fog by Thomas Hanna

Nine Mile Bridge by Helen Hamlin

In Maine by John N. Cole

The Cows Are Out! by Trudy Chambers Price

Hauling by Hand by Dean Lawrence Lunt

down the road a piece: A Storyteller's Guide to Maine by John McDonald

A Moose and a Lobster Walk into a Bar by John McDonald

At One: In a Place Called Maine by Lynn Plourde and Leslie Mansmann

The Little Fisherman by Margaret Wise Brown and Dahlov Ipcar

Titus Tidewater by Suzy Verrier

A is for Acadia by Richard Johnson and Ruth Gortner Grierson

These and other Maine books are available at:
www.islandportpress.com

A Maine Summer Island

The Story of Bustins

by F. Benjamin Carr

ISLANDPORT PRESS

ISLANDPORT PRESS • FRENCHBORO • YARMOUTH

ISLANDPORT PRESS
P.O. Box 10
Yarmouth, Maine 04096
www.islandportpress.com
books@islandportpress.com

Copyright © 2008 by F. Benjamin Carr

All Rights Reserved.

ISBN: 978-1-934031-15-5
Library of Congress Card Number: 2008929758

Book jacket design by Karen F. Hoots / Hoots Design
Book designed by Michelle A. Lunt / Islandport Press
Publisher Dean L. Lunt
Cover photo courtesy of Dean L. Lunt
Back cover photo courtesy of Freeport Historical Society

To My Father

A skilled and dedicated physician;
A gentle, patient, loving, and ever-supportive father;
A beacon whose beams still brighten my path.

To My Wife

In build, slight, in will and spirit, amazing;
Adventuresome, curious, intuitive;
Centered, serene, gracious;
Lover of her paints, family, and God's creation;
Heart of my heart.

Acknowledgments

WHEN A project has crept forward slowly over a considerable period of time, the chance grows that significant contributors will not be recognized. Many have aided me over the past decade—some with information and anecdotes, others with continuing encouragement. I am grateful for the assistance and support I have received in all its varied and valued forms.

George Richardson's *History of Bustins Island, Casco Bay, 1660–1960* has been a wellspring of information on the early years of summer folk on Bustins. Every rereading has provided new material overlooked in earlier readings. In addition, George and his wife, Connie, provided not only photographs and other illustrative material but also unflagging interest: "Is that book ever going to be published?"

Al and Sue Spalding have detailed memories covering the primary period this book chronicles. They provided insights into the operation of the Ships Inn during its final years and into the construction of the island ferry, the *Lilly B.* Sue, as clerk of the Bustins Island Village Corporation, graciously guided me through the corporation's well-maintained records. Both she and Al read early drafts of this book with critical eyes, as did Pam Canu.

Robbie Boone, Jean Whiting, the late Charlie Kitchin, the late Winnie Tozier, Ken Roberts, Harold Wade, and others shared remembrances of our unforgettable characters. Alice Forgit refreshed my memory of the musical life enlivening the island in the 1950s. Wally Baker shared an inclusive record on the electrification controversy. John Garfield reviewed the chapter on finances. Libby Silver shared a remembrance of Al Guppy's ferry. Both Len Larrabee and the late Bob Rudolph took time to write out their recollections of the laborious process leading to agreement with Freeport on the sharing of tax monies. Town manager Dale Olmstead reflected on the process from the town's perspective.

I gleaned much information from a wide spectrum of books, old and recent, too numerous to list in this book of tales. I am also grateful for the expert assistance I received from Jean Whiting, archivist of the Bustins Island Historical Society, and Randall Wade Thomas, director of the Freeport Historical Society. I thank others who also helped with this project, not least the hardworking staff and publisher Dean Lunt at Islandport Press. And as nearly every author does, I take ownership for any errors that readers may discover.

Ben Carr
Hancock, Maine
May 2008

Table of Contents

	Prologue: Going Home	xi
1	The Island	1
2	Island Education	13
	Glimpses: Spring	21
3	Rusticators	27
4	Ralph, Lilly and Archie	49
5	The Fifties	75
	Glimpses: Summer	89
6	An Electrifying Controversy	99
7	Financing a Summer Island	115
8	Regulation Comes to Bustins	131
9	Bustins Buys a Boat	141
10	My Community, Our Community	151
	Glimpses: Fall	161
	Epilogue: Time to Leave	167
	F. Benjamin Carr	171

Prologue

Going Home

"WHERE ARE you going?" asks a visitor at the South Freeport Town Landing. The man, waiting for his number to be called at Harraseeket Lunch so that he can pick up his fried clam platter at the window, is eyeing our duffels, L.L. Bean canvas totes, and coolers. They are piled below the harbormaster's crow's nest at the top of the gangplank.

"We're going home," we answer.

That's explanation enough, as far as we are concerned. We know soon our ferry will ease us out through Harraseeket Harbor, slide between Wolfe's Neck and Pound of Tea Island and cross two miles of open Casco Bay water before nudging gently against the Public Dock on our little Bustins Island, barely three-quarters of a mile long by one-third mile wide. Soon after we will unpack bags and put food in the fridge in our cottage, one of more than one hundred such summer cottages that sit tooth-to-jowl, lining the island's edge like a multicolored necklace.

Like us, many islanders—summer residents all—view Bustins Island as home. Granted, such a view does not arise overnight nor perhaps exist in the mind of island youth. Certainly it was not in my mind as a youngster. My memories of first coming to Bustins Island as a six-year-old in 1939 have much more to do with a long ride and the inevitable, "Are we almost there?"

It was June—we always visited in June because my father, a young physician in Worcester, Massachusetts, needed to vacation

A Maine Summer Island: The Story of Bustins

Courtesy of Marilyn Carr

Dorothea Carr, Ben's mother, reading on the island rocks in 1939 in a photo taken by his father.

early each summer so physicians with more seniority could vacation in the coveted months of July and August. After years of driving Fords, my father had just bought his first Buick, a gray two-door sedan with sporty blue wheel-trim accented with thin pencil stripes of yellow, but lacking one costly extra—a radio. Our car was packed to the roof with suitcases, food, balls, bats, my parents, me, and Calvin, my younger brother.

We traveled narrow country roads from Worcester through Concord until finally joining Route 1 near the Massachusetts coastal town of Newburyport. Then came exciting moments while I tried to distract or sit on my brother, subtly enough to avoid parental ire, so I could be the first to say—"I see Grandpa's water tower" when I spied the huge mushroom-shaped storage tank he had built and which stood out on the Newburyport skyline. Soon, we crossed the Merrimack River and drove on through Portsmouth, New Hampshire, and Maine coastal towns and cities until finally, with rain threatening, we reached Freeport.

We were to meet Ralph "Robbie" Robinson, the alumni secretary at Worcester Academy who had sailed to the Arctic with Captain Donald MacMillan on the schooner *Bowdoin*. Robbie was a patient of my father's and, most importantly, owned a cottage on Bustins Island. We drove back and forth several times past the designated meeting place at the corner of Bow and South streets before realizing that the man hunched over on a rock reading a newspaper, raincoat buttoned, and hat brim hiding his face, was Robbie.

Then it was on to South Freeport. We turned left down Main Street with its modest Cape Cod–style houses and overarching elm trees, and down the hill to the dock with its strange new smells of bait, tar, low tide, and fuel. Unpainted shacks and sheds leaned at odd angles. Lobster-fishing boats lay close by and the dock was strewn with the inevitable untidy piles of gear, its use unclear to us.

In the midst of all these new sights, sounds and smells lay the ferry *Spindrift* with Captain John Jaynes waiting on the dock beside her. He was slight of build with thinning hair, an aquiline nose, and alert blue eyes behind large, thick-lensed glasses. He had been engineer on a number of MacMillan's trips north on the *Bowdoin*, and he and Robbie knew one another well. Quickly we loaded suitcases and gear, cast off, and headed out toward a distant and enticing Bustins Island, mysterious in the late afternoon haze. I hardly knew what to expect.

The *Spindrift* slid in toward the Public Dock adjacent to the strange architectural landmark I came to know as the Nubble. Our luggage was unloaded from the deck of the boat and piled in the open rear of the Model A that had come to John through his in-laws, the Barnards. I was wide-eyed, a new world opening before me. As the Model A disappeared up the dirt road, Robbie walked us to the Wade cottage, named the Universal Joint, where we joined the Wade children for an island supper. Presiding at the table were the inimitable Meta and Bill Wade (another of my father's patients in Worcester as well as headmaster of Worcester Academy). By supper's end my stomach was full and my eyelids heavy. Paul Wade, youngest of the Wade offspring, and I made our way to the upstairs sleeping porch. I was asleep almost instantly. I hardly had time to realize that it was the first night I had ever slept outside or on an island.

The next morning we moved down a few doors to Robbie's cottage where we settled in for two weeks on the island. My mother and father spent their time reading on the upthrust ledges in what many call Kitchin's Cove, while Calvin and I braved the barnacled rocks, seaweed, and cold water. We walked to the six-hole golf course and watched the men banter back and forth. Each day we awakened early to the distinctive sounds of one-lunger lobster boats tending traps in Casco Bay. We dug clams with Robbie for chowder, delicious beyond imagination, that he himself made.

F. Benjamin Carr

Courtesy of Ben Carr
Young Ben Carr Jr. with his mother, Dorothea, and his father, Ben.

A highlight of each day was the mail boat, *Tourist*. It arrived from Portland with protesting hisses and screeches from its steam engine and a belch of black smoke from its tall stack. We waited in a little shed on the steamer dock, its walls an island "Who's Who" of carved initials and youthful island love. Joining us were the few others then on the island; some of them, like the leather-faced Art Henderson and the cherubic-looking Lew Ward, taking a break from whatever cottage maintenance tasks they had been doing. We were glad to visit with them, of course, but we had more serious business at hand. We didn't expect mail, but we did expect our daily delivery of H.P. Hood milk from Portland, eight or ten miles away by water. My mother, a stickler on such matters, spent weeks before our trip to the island arranging with

Courtesy Bustins Island Historical Society

John Jaynes and his famous Model A Ford. Going along for the ride are: Ruth Swan, Jane Ricker, Ethel Swan.

people at Hoods to deliver milk, well-iced, to the steamer each morning. She wanted us to have the same milk on vacation that we found each morning on our back porch at home. Apparently the Hoods people knew better than to disregard my mother's wishes.

On ice delivery days we waited for Ralph Brewer to bring huge cakes of ice for our ice chest. (Ralph never stopped long; maybe the lemonade we offered was not strong enough for his taste!) Our stove was fueled by kerosene. From the drum on the back porch we filled a glass jug, which, placed upside down like a plasma bottle, allowed the kerosene to gurgle-gurgle into the stove. The red hand pump by the sink provided water, heated on the stove, for baths in the big tub upstairs. An ingenious feed system existed to get hot water upstairs without using kettles and buckets, but we never mastered it. In the evening we all read, as best we could, by kerosene and Aladdin lamps—the latter dangerous because the flame always crept up until it came out the chimney-top. Since the house had been used as a dormitory in the days of MacMillan's summer nautical camp Wychmere, it had many bedrooms. My brother and I had vied for front rooms; I as the older had won. Besides, my folks wanted Calvin closer to their bedroom so they could monitor his sleep. He was only two, after all, while I was a much more manly six.

One day we went to Christmas Cove where we sailed—briefly—on the *Bowdoin* with MacMillan just before the ship left for Greenland. I remember enjoying the gumdrops intended for children of the north more than I remember Captain Mac. But on most days the Wade cottage acted as a magnet. I found it endlessly fascinating to watch Junie and Alan, the older Wade boys, blistering old paint off the side of their cottage with a blowtorch. They used the same approach to prepare their Pow-Wow class sailboat, *Stormalong*, for paint as they got it ready for launching and an exciting sailing season. Sailing these Pow-Wows—built in Amesbury, Massachusetts, and costing $450 new— was "hilarious, fun, wild and wet," according to islander Stuart MacDonald.

If my timing was good—and my nose was my trustworthy sleuth—I might be offered a fresh hot doughnut just emerging from the heavy fat-filled skillet on Meta Wade's kerosene stove. She was famous far and wide for her afternoon doughnuts, and many other accomplishments as well. Tiny and quick of speech, she was a prolific creator of children's stories. Most of them—in strange contrast to their refined author—gory and featuring vicious villains. After our doughnuts, we always tried to persuade her to tell us a story or two—not a difficult task. She would bring shivers to our spines with a tale, or teach us such unladylike phrases as "knuckle sandwich," "fist-full of five," and "I'll knock your grub-tooth down your gangplank."

Then Paul Wade and I would slide away to find Johnny Smoker, a little older than us but about the only other playmate on the island so early in the season. We trampled down the high grass in Dr. Eugster's backyard to create our ball field. We skulked around the docks, explored tide pools, checked the different paths through the woods, and peered into cottage windows. Johnny's folks ran the summer store and lived in Rocky Ledge right across from it. Our Bustins days could not end before Johnny's father, Eugene, received the store's first delivery of summer ice cream. The first cone of the summer—invariably black raspberry for me—somehow always tasted better than any other cone that followed.

All too soon, it was time for my family to pack suitcases, close the doors and windows of the cottage, and head back to a more ordinary summer in Worcester.

We returned to Bustins in 1940 and 1941. Since we were the first cottage users of the season, we always found the grass long. We spent the first two days with scythe and sickle getting the grass down to a level where, with our blisters bandaged, we could cut it with the hand mower, working in and around the granite cropping out through the grass at so many points. I remember numerous trips back and forth to South Freeport on John Jaynes's boats. Most people were either Jaynes people or Guppy people. The Guppys, a longtime island family, ran a competing ferryboat. We were Jaynes people and, with children's unswerving loyalty, ridiculed the Guppy boats and Guppy people. As many youngsters before and after me, I fancied myself a crewman and baggage handler. Guy Curit worked for Jaynes, and I worked hard to make him my friend. Eventually he permitted me to stand on an overturned wooden milk box and steer the *Spindrift* out in the open water. The *Cadet*, built by the navy in 1886, was the ancient "workboat" of the Jaynes fleet and too temperamental for me to touch. It was also much slower than the *Spindrift;* just another reason to always hope the *Spindrift* would be the ferry on a given day. Once with the Wades we took a day trip on the *Spindrift* to Seguin Island and walked up to

F. Benjamin Carr

Courtesy of Dean L. Lunt

The Lookout, Ben and Marilyn's cottage on the east side of Bustins Island. The original cottage was built in 1913.

the lighthouse that was then manned by keepers eager for visitors with news from ashore.

World War II interrupted our Bustins trips, as it interrupted the life patterns for so many families. A fellow physician had persuaded my father to join the Navy Reserve in 1935, long before anyone thought much of war. To his surprise my father was called to active duty in April of 1941, eight months before Pearl Harbor. During the war he was stationed in various places, and we followed him as he found housing for us. We had a splendid summer on the Lake Michigan shore while he was stationed at Great Lakes, and then, for over two years we lived in San Francisco while he served in the Pacific as a navy doctor.

After the war, we returned to Worcester and visited Bustins again in the summers of 1946 and 1947. Memories crowd in from those years when I was a young teenager. Of course, we still received our Hoods milk each day. I remember rowing with Paul Wade to the Whale's Belly, a well-furnished two-story treehouse on the west side of Big Whaleboat Island. Over several years, Johnny Smoker, Jiffy Drew, Al Spalding, Ken Roberts, and the Wolf brothers had built the treehouse from the top down with all sorts of scavenged materials and furnishings. My most vivid memory of the adventure centers around a long dark night there being eaten alive by mosquitoes—and then having to row all the way back to Bustins the next morning. My parents were pretty protective of their sons, and I have never understood why they let me go on that expedition; it seemed so unlike them. Perhaps they didn't know how far we were rowing. Perhaps Paul's parents talked them into it. Who knows!

I remember climbing onto the porch roof of White Cap cottage with Paul and finding an unlocked window that let us enter and snoop around. I remember helping Lilly Brewer sweep out the dusty Blaisdell cottage (now Dr. Steve Drew's cottage) and being full of sneezes for the next three days. I remember beating the bushes around the golf course with Anne Wade, looking for lost balls that we washed and sold to needy golfers. I remember lots of tennis with my father on the island's minimally maintained courts. I remember cribbage at night (fifteen-two and fifteen-four!) and, just at bedtime, a root beer float made with heavy cream rather than ice cream, and kept cold with ice chipped from the block in the fridge.

I especially remember the summer of 1947 with its after-dark games of kick the can and capture the flag. At fourteen, I had just finished my first year at Worcester Academy and had discovered girls. Like iron filings drawn to a magnet, I was pulled to a newcomer, Mickey, staying just two cottages away. She climbed trees like a squirrel, ran like a gazelle, was slender and pretty with long dark hair and big brown eyes. As we got to know one another, we found we were never captured during the games—it was much more exciting to hide together beneath the drooping branches of a fir tree where we exchanged tentative kisses, oblivious to the games raging around us. All too soon, especially that year, my family was Worcester-bound again. Mickey and I promised to write and made the other kinds of promises young people in love make to one another. We kept those promises for a time until we were caught up again in our other lives. Our letters slowed and finally stopped.

Our family didn't return to Bustins after 1947 because, perhaps inspired by our wartime journeys and caught up in the American romance with the open road, we traveled for our vacations—to the south, to Canada, to the Grand Canyon, the Blue Ridge Mountains, and Crater Lake.

In fact, my parents never visited Bustins together again. While my mother lived to be ninety-six and frequently spent time on the island in later years, she came alone. My father died at a relatively young age.

Courtesy of Marilyn Carr

Marilyn's son Kim and our grandson Sammy at the rope swing on the east side, 2006.

A Maine Summer Island: The Story of Bustins

As children on Bustins, my brother and I could do things with our parents—swim, boat, read, golf, tennis, baseball—without our father always being called away to office hours or medical meetings or to call on the sick, or to attend church meetings. Islands attract people, in part, because they promise freedom from the tyranny of time. It was a special family time. I felt a certain pride in knowing what to expect and how to find my way around. I knew how to get from the Community House to the steamer dock by the woods path, how to make the pitcher pumps work, and when to expect the ferries and steamers. I knew about tides and clams. More importantly, I knew the people. I had grown to love the island even if I was not yet consciously ready to call it "home."

Over the next two decades I visited Bustins sporadically and usually off-season until the 1960s, aided by my old friend Lilly Brewer. I returned and renewed my love affair with the island and with the brown-eyed young tomboy now grown to a lovely and gracious woman, an accomplished painter in oil and watercolor. She had an avid interest in depicting coastal scenes then; later she turned to close-ups of nature in its many forms, especially flowers and shells. She had recently bought a small cottage, The Lookout, which had been built about 1913 or so and was located amidst birches and oaks down at the northeast corner of the island. She loved the island and so did I for its natural beauty, for its determinedly rustic ways that were so different from what we encountered ashore, for its people with whom we seemed to share so much in common, for its link to our childhoods, and for a myriad of other reasons. In time we married and moved to Maine full-time in the early 1970s. We were fortunate enough to find positions in public education, I as a high school principal and Marilyn (as Mickey had grown into) as an art teacher. We lived in Addison and North Berwick while I was principal of local high schools. Marilyn taught in Columbia Falls and Cherryfield and then became a K–12 art teacher in Machias, the first public school art teacher in Washington County. Later she taught for a number of years at Massabesic Junior High School in Waterboro.

As long as the calendars of our respective school districts matched, and they usually did, our first Bustins week of the year coincided with April vacation. The ferry didn't run out of season, so in the early to mid-seventies Bud Nickerson in his broad-bottomed skiff ferried us with our necessaries and two collies, Heather and Bonnie, from Flying Point in Freeport to the rocks below our cottage. He would head off, promising to collect us the next Sunday. In later years, Charlie Kitchin provided our transport. He would meet us at Roland and Georgia Gateses' home on Flying Point where he had his outhaul, and later at his own home on the back of the Point. The tides governed our coming and going; always we had to cross with the water above mid-tide to avoid the mudflats that appeared as the tide fell.

"How are you two lovebirds doing?" Charlie would greet us.

April weather can be chancy and changeable: cold or less cold, windy or calm, wet or dry—usually all the above. Seldom did we find consistent stretches of fair weather in that season. Enough warmth to entice us to eat our lunch down on the dock made for a memorable day. It was a week for opening the cottage, getting the water system hooked up and working, for walking and reading, for watching the birds over the water and in the trees, for raking leaves and dead grass if the yard was dry enough, for just being together. We rested from the winter rigors of school life and geared up for the last push to Memorial Day and then beyond to the end of the school year.

A Maine Summer Island: The Story of Bustins

During these Bustins days we were free from school opening and closing hours, the search for substitute teachers, bus problems, the preparation for meetings, the deadlines for this or that report, the rules and regulations that generally ordered our lives. We were free from everything except the tide, which dictated when

Marilyn and Ben Carr in the 1970s.

Courtesy of Ben Carr

F. Benjamin Carr

we could—or could not—get across those mudflats. Marilyn could paint; I could read and reflect. We could read aloud as we have done throughout our marriage. We could enjoy the natural world with its own rhythms: when the first migratory birds gradually filtered in to take their places amongst those which had never left; when the rockweed began to change color and the eelgrass to grow; when the water table began to recede. We reveled in the sight of trees beginning to bud. We were awed when the moon approached or had passed full with resultant monster high tides and drainer lows. This was the season when mother seals would haul out on the ledges with their offspring. It was the season when we gathered with other early visitors like Bud and Olive Nickerson, the Gateses, and Lilly Brewer for potluck suppers. We would pass around a book of Robert Service's poetry, each person reading aloud under the wavering gaslight. Lilly's never-changing favorite was "The Ballad of the Ice-Worm Cocktail." They were memorable evenings. Through them all, even though we knew we shared the island with others, we always considered it "ours."

The years have flown by since then. Yellow school buses and a calendar dictated by school terms and school holidays are a distant memory. Propane gas—at ever higher prices—continues to fuel our Bustins fridge, hot water heater, stove, and some lights. But we also have insulated The Lookout to make it more comfortable over a longer season, and we have installed solar panels on the roof to keep batteries charged and to provide the direct-current electricity that powers a few lights, a small television, and—those symbols of our age—a laptop computer and a cell phone. We look forward to the visits of our shared children and grandchildren. We look forward to early-morning birding paddles in our ocean kayaks. We look forward to taking our lunch down the stairs to our little deck by the water. Often we move from lunch to a brief "PS"—"power snooze" to the uninitiated. Later we walk the dirt road that circles the island. At some point one of us will ask that time-honored island question, "How long does it take to walk around Bustins?" and the other answers, always thoughtfully, "It depends on whom you meet." And then we laugh as though hearing the joke for the first time.

We watch the sparkle on the water as cats'-paws of breeze riffle its surface. We watch the games of Ultimate Frisbee on the golf course in the evening. Anyone who wishes to play does; families, including our children and grandchildren, eat dinner early to be ready for the evening contest at 7:00 p.m. Perhaps a thunderstorm rumbles through in the early evening, and later, before bed and with the storm past, we reach for a handful of stars seemingly close enough to grab. A great horned owl calls in the dark morning hours; we listen for a muted response from the next island.

We attend the annual bean supper on the Fourth of July, we take friends to see this year's exhibit at the Ships Inn Museum, and we gather in the Community House on August's first Saturday for the annual meeting of the Bustins Island Village Corporation, and before we know it, another season has passed. We say good-bye to dear friends and wish them a healthy and happy winter. We are all conscious of time's passage, of changes in our own lives as we age. But through it all we still think of Bustins as "ours," not simply as a comfortable refuge but as "home," the place where we feel most rooted. Returning to the island after an absence is like being reunited with a lover after time apart. All our senses are alert; we are ready to love anew, to reaffirm our commitment.

So when the man "from away" at the dock those many years ago asked "Where are you going?", our answer was both natural and without artifice or airs. "We're going home."

Chapter One

The Island

CASCO Bay encompasses two hundred square miles from its more westerly tip at Cape Elizabeth to its more easterly tip at Cape Small. Lonely, wave-wracked Halfway Rock and its lighthouse mark the midpoint of a line connecting the two Capes. Six rivers, none major, flow into the bay. Within its bounds three ranges of islands run in southwesterly directions contributing their share to what are commonly called the Calendar Islands. To actually count 365 islands and justify the name, numerous ledges exposed only at low tide need be included in the tally, along with barren rocks inhabited only by nesting birds.

Bustins Island lies in a quiet corner of inner Casco Bay, amidst a string of small islands southwest of Mere Point, just a mile or two offshore from South Freeport and Wolfe's Neck, even closer to Flying Point, and with a distant view of Portland Harbor about 10 miles away. Composed, like most Casco Bay islands, of granite and layers of metamorphic rock thrust up by ancient volcanic action to lie on edge, the island is perhaps three-quarters of a mile long and one-third of a mile wide, 138 acres in size. The island's highest point is 83 feet above sea level where clumps of moss conceal the granite and rampant tree growth blocks most views. Today the island has a thin ground cover supporting an army of conifers with, at its northeast end, a mix of hardy old oaks and some maple and birch trees. A dirt road encircles the island and occasional crossroads and paths cut through the

A Maine Summer Island: The Story of Bustins

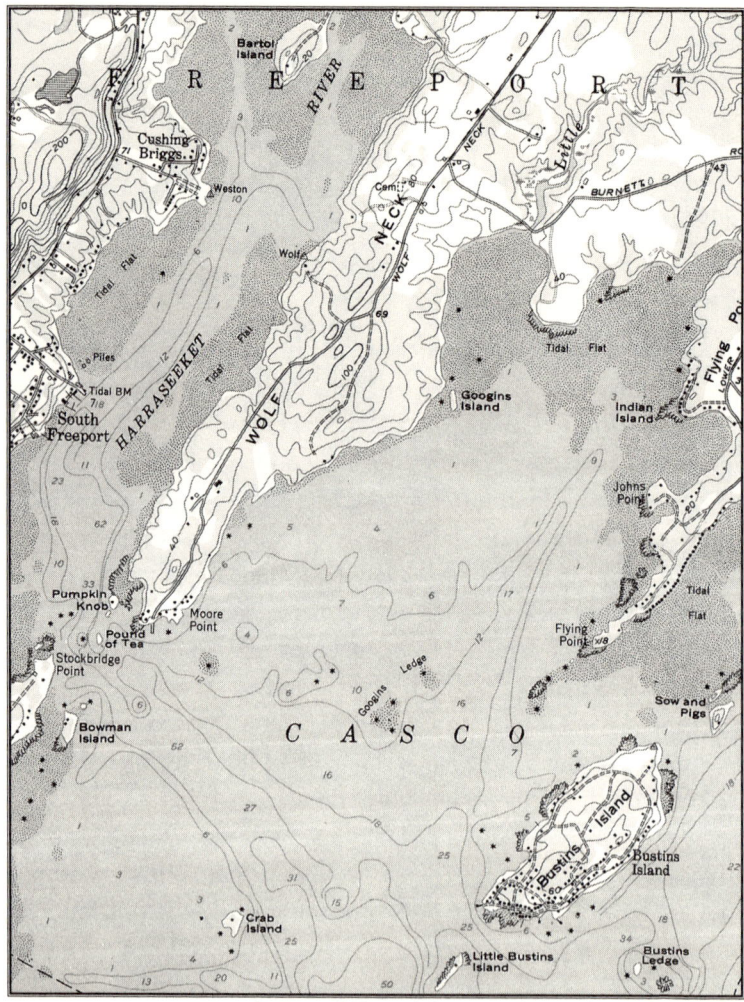

Courtesy of National Oceanic and Atmospheric Administration
A chart of Bustins Island and Freeport.

island's midsection. A handful of island-owned vehicles provide essential services, but private vehicles are prohibited. Somewhat over one hundred seasonal cottages, mostly modest in size and simply constructed in the country style of a century ago, lie close-packed, side by side along the water's edge. Most islanders use propane gas for cooking, refrigeration, and lighting. Some also use kerosene lamps, and some, electricity provided by solar panels. All of this in the absence of island electricity. Many cottages still use outhouses, though many others have installed various forms of "modern" facilities. All of the cottages are shuttered in the winter.

The record of the island's earliest history is minimal. Early records list fur trader John Bustion as owning Bustions Island in 1660. He sold it to a William Haines of Pine Point—present-day Flying Point—in 1667. If this is the earliest mention of our Bustins Island, it came at a time when many surrounding islands and rivers were also finding first mention and being named. In 1636, William Royall occupied a point of land in what is now Yarmouth, and gave his name to the Royal River. In the same

Courtesy of Robert Boone

An aerial view of Bustins Island taken in 1939.

A Maine Summer Island: The Story of Bustins

Collection of Freeport Historical Society

Bustins Island in the early 1900s looking south toward Chebeague Island.

year, George Jewell, for some gunpowder, rum, and a few fishhooks, bought from the local tribes the island that bears his name. In 1645, John Cousins bought two islands, which are now called Cousins and Littlejohn islands. In 1658, Hugh Moshier settled in the area and bought the two islands that bear his name. Henry Wolf married the daughter of Thomas Sheppard who lived on the point of land between Bustins and the Harraseeket Harbor, a point known successively as Harraseeket Neck, Sheppard's Point, and finally Wolfe's Neck.

By the late seventeenth century, the era of stability and relative peace in the region drew to a close. A succession of wars ensued. Some grew out of wars being waged in Europe that overflowed into the New World. Others were more local in their beginnings. But whatever their origins, these wars caused widespread disruption and loss of life. The first of these wars has been called King Philip's War, named after the Pokanoket sachem the English called Philip. He was the son of Massasoit who had helped the Pilgrims who landed in Plymouth in 1620. The fighting that began in southern New England in time spread to Maine. Many settlers were driven from their homes in the ensuing hostilities. In 1676, a significant number sought refuge on Jewell Island and other islands. When these islands turned out to be vulnerable, coming under attack from canoe-borne Abenakis, the settlers fled to southern New England. Unrest in the Casco Bay area continued, lasting through the War of Independence.

In 1700, since so many records and title deeds were destroyed in attacks and burnings, the General Court of Massachusetts, then in control of Maine, appointed a committee to sort out land claims by residents of the district. Their findings, reached over many years, were recorded in the Book of Eastern Claims. Amongst them is a claim by Francis Haines, son of the late William Haines, for the land held by his father at Pine Point and Bustions Island. Haines claimed that his father had improved the lands—a very significant test for ownership—and "had several children born in the said place . . . the said claimer being one of them." Despite supporting testimony by former neighbors, including the fact of John Bustion's death forty years earlier in 1673, the claim was not honored. Francis Haines died about 1715 without regaining his family land.

In 1722, the governor signed an order granting a petition to the General Court of Massachusetts by both resident and nonresident proprietors of North Yarmouth, of which the Freeport area was then a part. That petition requested the appointment of a five-person committee to oversee the resettlement of the town and its business affairs. The committee members were all men of status in the Massachusetts colony. Perhaps most prominent was John Powell, married to the sister of the Massachusetts lieutenant governor William Dummer. Powell moved from Boston to North Yarmouth where he pursued the committee's work energetically.

By 1738, the task was completed, and in appreciation the members were given lands in the northeastern part of town to be divided amongst them. John Powell received "Bustain Island" and another small island known as Basket Island. He died in 1742; his son Jeremiah Dummer Powell inherited the island. Though title to the island was held over many years—Jeremiah lived until 1784—it is unlikely that any of the Powell family ever lived on the island.

A chart of Casco Bay, drawn for the British Admiralty and published in London in 1776, showed not only the islands but also houses and farms. A few houses and farms are shown on Flying Point, as well as two houses on Lower Goose Island, a number on Chebeague and Cousins islands, and a number on Harpswell, but nothing on Bustins Island.

At the time of the war, Freeport was a newly settled section of the older established North Yarmouth. In 1789, Freeport was separated from North Yarmouth and incorporated as the sixty-fourth town in Maine. As part of the separation, Freeport received not only a number of small islands near shore, but also Southworth, Crab, Bustins, Little Bustins, Sow and Pigs, French, Pettengill, Williams, and Sisters islands.

Eight years later, on December 15, 1797, a significant entry appears in the Cumberland County Registry of Deeds. It pertains to the estate of Jeremiah Powell and is taken by his wife as executrix of his estate. "In consideration of $300 paid by James Bibber of Freeport, County of Cumberland, the receipt of whereof I do hereby acknowledge," the entry reads, "have and do by these present, give, grant, sell and convey unto him, the said James Bibber, his heirs forever, 'Bustians Island,' so called, formerly situated in North Yarmouth but now of Freeport, aforesaid

F. Benjamin Carr

containing by estimation eighty acres. This property was acquired by me through lawful inheritance."

    A James Bibber, born in 1706 on the Isle of Jersey in the English Channel Islands off the coast of France, came to New England in 1722, according to the vital records of Phippsburg, Maine. He married Abigail Drew of Dover, New Hampshire, and they had a large family. He died in Harpswell in 1773. One of their children was James, born in 1753. James served four enlistments in the colonial militia and survived the disastrous expedition to the Penobscot in 1777, described as probably the worst naval defeat suffered by the United States Navy until Pearl Harbor. He married Johanna Bailey and they had thirteen children, including Bailey Bibber and a daughter Susanne. It was James and Johanna who bought Bustians Island in 1797 and began building a farmhouse the next year. Oxen, driven across the ice or ferried from Harpswell, helped clear the land and dig a cellar hole the length of the house. The countless rocks and boulders unearthed in the clearing process were used to wall the cellar. The Bibber farmhouse (owned by the Kitchin family for many years) still stands as the oldest structure on the island.

    Little is known of the Bibber family and their lives on Bustins, though they made their livelihood for more than fifty years by farming and fishing. Certainly they kept animals. The island was primarily pastureland, especially through the center section. Probably the Bibbers practiced a mixed husbandry. He may have fished and fashioned ax handles, shingles, or barrel staves from island lumber. She took care of the garden crops, the cows, the oxen, the pigs if any, the sheep, and the children. She may also have raised flax to be spun, together with wool from the sheep, into linsey-woolsey for clothing the family. One way or another it must have been a lonely life, distant from neighbors and markets. It surely was backbreaking work—clearing, planting, trying to eke out enough to care for the family, and to pay bills and taxes.

But the advantages of island life should not be overlooked. The waters of Casco Bay were slow to cool in the fall and provided a longer growing season. Natural fertilizers were at hand: seaweed, for instance, and lobsters—more nuisance than delicacy in those years—and pogies. Wresting a subsistence living from the soil could be supplemented by fishing. The struggle bred the sense of self-reliance and ingenuity for which Yankee farmers were known.

The Bibbers' daughter Susanne married John Johnson who resided variously in Cumberland, Durham, and Falmouth. On March 12, 1834, James and Johanna sold the island to their son-in-law for $1,000. "Bustins Island, so called," the deed reads, "containing eighty acres, more or less, also one yoke of oxen, three cows, one two year old heifer, and one yearling bull and twenty sheep, also all the farming tools, ploughs, harrows, chains, cars, sleds, pitch forks, shovels and hoes. This deed conveys all the buildings on same island except the house and lot owned by my son Bailey Bibber."

In 1843, James Bibber died at the age of ninety. George Richardson's *History of Bustins Island Casco Bay 1660–1960*, relates the story passed down by a great-granddaughter of the Bibbers that James, Johanna, and one of the children were buried on Bustins. Three upright weathered stones with no apparent markings may pinpoint their resting place on the Shore Reserve between the present Dennett and Wade cottages. On the Sunday of Labor Day Weekend 1992, descendants of the Bibbers gathered before these stones for a brief service of remembrance. During it I exhorted family and gathered islanders to reflect on the linkages of freedom with struggle, commitment, and sacrifice both in James Bibber's day and in our own. A Revolutionary War marker was placed in the ground. During most summers a small American flag, commemorating James Bibber's service to his country, now flutters in the breeze beside the largest stone.

In 1854, John and Susanne Johnson, listed as living in Falmouth, sold their portion of Bustins Island for $1,500 to Elisha Stover of Harpswell. The sale included another small island named Little Bustins. The wood on the small island, however, was retained by John Johnson.

In 1856, the Bibbers' son, Bailey, and his wife Dorothy of Harpswell mortgaged their island farmhouse to David Coffin of Freeport for $100. The property was described as being bounded by the waters of Casco Bay and the lands of Elisha Stover and "being same occupied by me for forty-five years past, and formerly owned by James Bibber, since deceased." The following spring the same property was deeded back to Bibber. Perhaps the whole arrangement was designed simply to ease Bailey Bibber through a difficult financial shortfall.

During these years Casco Bay and Maine were bustling. Fishing was a primary industry and nearby South Freeport, early known as Strout's Point, was a center of that industry in the

Courtesy of Dean L. Lunt
A front view of the Bibber farmhouse, built in 1798 on the island's east side. The house remains the oldest structure on the island.

Courtesy of Ben Carr

Ben Carr, far right, presides over the dedication of a Revolutionary War marker commemorating James Bibber. The marker is located in front of the Wade cottage. Observers from left to right are: Joan Henziker, Charlotte Maurer, Clarence Wall, Marge Wall, Kim Ryan, the Bibbers, Charlie Kitchin, Jean Whiting, and Ben Carr.

early nineteenth century. Many important products were handled there, including lumber, potash, pitch, and furs. But fish topped the list. Twelve thousand barrels of mackerel were packed at Strout's Point in and around 1812, for instance.

Along with fishing, shipbuilding and maritime commerce were important in Freeport. For years small vessels were built in the area for fishing, coastal trade, and occasionally for longer voyages—to the West Indies, for example. These vessels carried fish, of course, and firewood and a variety of other commodities from place to place (not least because roads were so abysmal). But shipbuilding in the Freeport area became increasingly important as the nineteenth century progressed. During the first half of the century Mast Landing and Porter's Landing were the most important villages in Freeport because of their commercial activity and access to the sea. Nearly all freight going to Center Village was unloaded at Porter's Landing. It was also home to an early steamer that began running to various points in Casco Bay in 1822. Captain Seward Porter installed a steam engine in a flat-bottomed scow and named his steamer the *Kennebec*, though she was more popularly known as the "Ground Hog" because of her propensity for running aground when her engine failed.

When railroad tracks, laid along the route deemed most topographically favorable, passed through hitherto less important Center Village, its preeminence was assured at the expense of Mast Cove and Porter's Landing. July 5, 1849, marked the first passenger trip on the Kennebec and Portland Railroad between Bath and Yarmouth. Passengers transferred to another train in Yarmouth to complete the trip to Portland. By 1874 four passenger trains, two to eight cars each, and two freight trains traveled in each direction daily. Passenger service through Center Village—the Freeport of today—continued into the 1950s.

Out in the bay, Henry F. Merrill joined with Edwin Morse of Bunganuc at the head of Maquoit Bay to purchase Bustins in 1876 from Elisha Stover. Merrill fought with the famed 20th Maine Regiment in the Civil War, during which he was captured and survived imprisonment at the notorious Andersonville Prison in Georgia. In 1877, the two men divided the island. Merrill lived in a farmhouse (owned by the Grece family today) across from where the island store would one day be built. His farm animals grazed peacefully, he raised some crops, and he probably fished for flounder and cunner. In 1885, Charles and

Margaret Guppy and their six children lived with him for a year before building their own house (today the Nielsen cottage). Merrill's brothers and father would take over most of his holdings in 1883, although he continued to live in the farmhouse.

The Morse holdings were repurchased by Stover in 1880 and sold the next year to Captain Henry Horr, who, with his family, lived in the Bibber farmhouse. Horr, in turn, would sell the holdings to Benjamin Swett in 1891. The Horrs had come from another island in Portland Harbor. During the fishing season Captain Horr might be gone in his sloop for several days at a time. Soon his son Levi built a cottage on the west side of the island. Later it was incorporated into today's Adams cottage. Nearby his brothers William and Jake built one- and two-room dwellings, marked by sharply pitched roofs, where they and their families lived until the mid-1890s surrounded by their fishing gear and the crops they grew to see themselves through the long winter. Two cellar holes mark the location of these early houses. About this same time a Chadwick family occupied the house, which is today's Martin cottage.

However, by the early 1890s, when the first summer cottages were built, the Merrill and Swett families owned essentially the whole island.

Chapter Two

Island Education

BUSTINS was part of the Town of Freeport, which bore responsibility for, among other things, education that in 1875 had been made compulsory for children aged seven to seventeen. In 1883 enrollment in the grammar school in South Freeport was so small during the spring that its students were combined with those in another school to save money. The same money-saving scheme was followed in the fall of the year. "We saved about $115 by the move," reported the supervisor, Mr. Burr, "more than enough to give a term of twelve weeks to the Islands."

A "small but very satisfactory" term was taught by George Hughey, who instructed six students on Bustins. He was paid $5.50, a week or $66 for the term. This is the first mention of formal schooling on the island. Henry Horr was paid $8.75 for cutting and fitting firewood for the school, no doubt located in his farmhouse.

Burr's successor, Edwin C. Thompson, who held a variety of Freeport town offices during his career, noted continuation of the school the next year, 1884, for "fourteen scholars in the various islands belonging to this town." During the single winter term offered, Hughey received the same stipend as before, but Horr was paid only $6.25 for his services.

In 1885, the supervisor picturesquely explained that money for schooling on Bustins could not be "judiciously expended" because "many of the inhabitants like the birds that fly round them, or swim in their waters, are migratory in their habits, moving from island to island, or place to place."

The island is not mentioned in the report for 1886, but in 1887, J. E. Hackett taught four Bustins students during an eleven-week winter term and was paid $66. A stove had been furnished and was in the charge of Henry Horr, who was paid $8 for rent and wood.

In 1888, voters at the annual Freeport Town Meeting approved $200 to build a schoolhouse on Bustins. In the next year's Annual Report are recorded disbursements, dated December 15, 1888, of $155 to M. D. Palmer for construction of the school, $1.80 to the steamer *Phantom*'s agent for a table and chair, and, on February 9, 1889, $6 to George Uniacke for a stove. The schoolhouse, 14 feet wide and 22 feet long, was completed for $162.80, leaving an unexpended balance of $37.20. The supervisor called the new school "well built, pleasant and comfortable. The pupils can now have the same privilege as other children of the town." Shirley Pettengill was the first teacher in the new schoolhouse and taught a winter term of twelve weeks.

Unfortunately, we do not know exactly where the school was located. An early photograph shows it in an open setting on a little knoll with a ledge breaking through the grass in the foreground. Perhaps this was on the west side close to the fishermen's houses. Or maybe it was near the old farmhouse in which instruction previously occurred. With the island so heavily wooded today, it is difficult to visualize the schoolhouse's location in the open surroundings of the photograph.

In 1889, both a spring and a winter term of ten weeks were held. Cora G. Hamilton taught the first, being paid $55 for her work with six "scholars." And Willard P. Hamilton received $62.50 for teaching seven "scholars" the second. Horr continued his custodial duties, receiving a total of $13.25. Townsend, the

F. Benjamin Carr

Collection of Edmund P. Skillin, Freeport Historical Society

The Bustins Island schoolhouse and pupils in the late 1800s or early 1900s. The schoolhouse, which still stands today, was built in 1888 and the final term took place in 1906.

supervisor, made it clear that he gave the same attention to the new island school as the other schools in town. "Although our visits were made unexpectedly, we always found the teachers and pupils at their work, and think they [the Hamiltons] were faithful in the discharge of their duties." The next year Will H. Tracy, whose wife Virgie was the local Freeport telephone operator, taught a spring term for seven enrollees. No winter term was held "on account of the scholars moving away."

No school term was held on Bustins in 1891 or 1892. But a short summer term of eight weeks was held in 1893, taught by Georgianna B. Sawyer, whose parents a year earlier had built Island View, the first summer cottage on Bustins.

The transient pupils demonstrated their transiency; no school was held in 1894 because of insufficient numbers. But in 1895 another summer session was begun on June 24 with Emma C. Sargent as teacher. The term, planned for ten weeks, was closed after seven because waves of whooping cough and scarlet fever raced through the student body.

The school reopened in 1896 and entered its period of greatest continuity and productivity under the teaching of Helen Dillingham of Bow Street in Freeport. She was valedictorian of her graduating class at Freeport High School in June of 1896 and met her eleven Bustins students for the first time on July 10. Because Dillingham missed the boat, her fall term with nine students opened a day late and ended on Friday, the last day of October. Following a two-week vacation, according to an article in the *Six Town Times*, she would attend the Normal School in Gorham. Dillingham returned in 1897 for a ten-week summer term. Ten students enrolled—everyone who was eligible, according to the supervisor's report—and attendance was nearly perfect. "There are some bright active pupils in this school, and in a few years we shall expect them to stand side by side in their school work with those on the main land."

F. Benjamin Carr

On September 4, 1897, the *Six Town Times* carried a report on the August 31 closing exercises of the school in which the students offered recitations and the reading of a Psalm. The family names of the presenters are familiar: Nan, Angeline, and Mary Martha Horr; Willy Horr; Charles Guppy; Margaret Swett (aunt of Nickie Kitchin and Bud Nickerson); and W. Horr.

In 1897, it was discovered that the schoolhouse was situated on land to which the town had no title. Furthermore, the owners of the land, to this day unidentified, notified the town to remove the schoolhouse since they were unwilling to sell the land to the town. In time the schoolhouse was moved to the parcel of land on which it still sits. This site was donated to the town by Josiah W. Merrill and his sons Josiah P. and William G. Merrill who had acquired most of Civil War veteran Henry Merrill's Bustins land. Before the Merrills made their generous gift, the issue was raised at Freeport's annual Town Meeting on March 14, 1898, with no reference to how or why the structure was initially built on land not belonging to the town. Perhaps the town had been given permission in 1888 to use land that was intended for a different use by 1898. Perhaps the increasing value of the land made it more desirable as a cottage site than as a school site. Although Bustins issues were understandably not as important to the town as mainland issues, it is difficult to believe that the town would have appropriated money for a schoolhouse without some assurance concerning the building site.

In any event, Joseph E. Davis offered—and his offer was accepted—to move the schoolhouse for $25. In time the move was made to the Merrill lot, "repairs made, seats added, and other work done, so that our Island pupils are as well cared for as those on the main." On August 13, 1898, the records indicate that J. E. Davis was paid $25 and C. H. Guppy $5, presumably for moving the school. The appropriation was overdrawn by $5.

Courtesy of Dean L. Lunt

The old schoolhouse in 2007. It was built in 1888.

On July 1, 1898, the *Six Town Times* reported that Miss Dillingham had gone to Bustins "to teach the school as usual." More than a dozen cottages had been built by this time and the new eager islanders were reconvening for the summer. Dillingham joined them for their first picnic of the season. The school on Bustins operated with summer and fall terms of ten weeks each for the children of the farmers and fishermen. It was open again in 1899 for a total of twenty-one weeks. Dillingham resigned her charge at the end of the summer term in order to finish her normal school course.

Dillingham was followed by Emma L. Soule, daughter of Mr. and Mrs. William F. Soule of Auburndale, Massachusetts, who built Norumbega, the present Hohn cottage on Bustins.

F. Benjamin Carr

In 1903, the school bell did not ring on Bustins. "Your Committee found it impossible to have teachers boarded at the Island and have had the scholars carried to South Freeport during such time as it was suitable. For the fall and winter terms board was provided at South Freeport and Porter's Landing for those who wished to attend school."

In 1904, Alice I. Gamman was paid $77 for teaching a spring term to nine students. In addition she received $2.50 for her janitorial work. In 1905, Laura S. Ring, whose family lived beyond the Flying Point school which later became the Thomas Means Club, rowed to the island each day to teach a spring term for six students. The June 22 *Casco Bay Breeze* praised the successful term under Ring, sister to the wife of Fred Pritham of Freeport who had helped build the Bustins roads and who was just graduating from medical school. Pritham worked as a general practitioner for sixty-five years in the Greenville area at the foot of Moosehead Lake.

The final term on Bustins was held in the spring of 1906 when seven students registered. A last lone entry in the town's Annual Report records that in 1907, Charles Guppy was paid $2.50 for wood.

As years passed, a summer community grew up around the deserted schoolhouse. The fishing families had left the island, the Maine Legislature passed an act in 1913 enabling the island to become a village corporation with a measure of self-autonomy, the Community House was completed in 1920 on land donated by the Merrill heirs, and the schoolhouse beside it was in time utilized as a generator house and storage area.

Today, the schoolhouse, one of Maine's smallest, remains in surprisingly good condition with its weathered exterior boards, small entry/cloak room, some original windows with wavy glass panes, and interior walls of plaster containing horsehair and crushed oyster shells as was the custom in the day when it was built. It remains as a reminder of the fiercely independent fishing families who used Bustins as a base and lived sometimes harsh, sometimes lonely lives along its shores. It remains as the island's only public building predating the development of the summer colony on Bustins. It also remains as a reminder of the ties, never tension-free, that for so long have bound Bustins and Freeport. Bustins folks have always grumbled about needs and expectations seemingly ignored or but partially met by the town. Freeporters, torn between feelings of obligation and the ever-expanding demands on available revenues, have provided just enough services to justify the perennial affirmation that the islanders have "the same privileges" as those on the mainland.

F. Benjamin Carr

Glimpses

Spring

Tendrils of smoke from our cottage chimney signaling efforts within to drive out the morning chill

The winter-fall of trees and branches strewn island-wide

Every brooklet at spate with foaming icy water rushing seaward

Early mayflowers in the hidden spots Nickie once showed us

Patches of hard snow behind shaded trees and crackly skim ice on ponds and road puddles

Courtesy of Linda Sweatt
Turtle Rock, one of the island's best known and popular landmarks.

Courtesy of Dean L. Lunt

Deep well hand pump outside a Bustins Island cottage. Some island cottages still draw their water using these types of hand pumps.

Charlie, muffled against the chill fingers of morning, rounding the point in *Pixie* with its ancient Johnson outboard

Roads still heaved up, fragile and crumbly from frost, waiting to be packed down by feet and tires

The island lying leafless and naked, its every curve revealed

F. Benjamin Carr

Rafts of eider ducks, cackling like hens, floating offshore

The lights of Flying Point at night seeming hardly beyond arm's length

Daffodils and forget-me-nots, early heralds of a season approaching with foot-dragging slowness

Day workers arriving on *Keep-ah* and *Foggy Notion*

The eagle flying toward French's Island, head and tail a flashing white in the late afternoon sun

Courtesy of Dean L. Lunt
The Nubble, another unique island landmark, located near the Public Dock.

A Maine Summer Island: The Story of Bustins

An artist's palette of soft greens as trees and shrubs finally burst winter's chains to bud and then leaf

The pristine whiteness of winter-scoured birch bark on the trinity at the edge of our bank

Delicate yellow clintonia blossoming beside the Morgan-Moore cottage

Blankets of bluets to be mowed around in the Eckel's backyard

The Kirkland float going in at a full-moon high tide

Great blue herons like statues-on-stilts fishing the mudflats at sunrise

Rhubarb, broad-leafed and red-stalked, ripening beside the Old Farmhouse

Members of the island family arriving on weekends to greet one another and open cottages

The smell of dry, musty, dusty old wood when first entering a winter-sealed cottage

Mouse nests cleaned from drawers, acorn shells swept from sheds

Pickup buoys replacing winter sticks offshore, and skiffs being patched and painted for the summer season

Storm shutters propped against sheds, bare windows as yet uncurtained, and no need for screens

F. Benjamin Carr

Courtesy of Dean L. Lunt
The former Ships Inn restaurant is now home to the Bustins Island Historical Society.

Charlie's Typhoon-class boat towed from Mere Point to be the first island sailboat on its mooring

The Carriers filling fire-truck tanks with water and setting out the Indian pumps and fire extinguishers

Day-Glo orange boundary pipes: George Richardson has sprayed his markers again

The sound of individual raindrops drumming against my skylight during a spring shower

Crawford and Rob Taisey taking time out from repairs on their old barn to be sure all fire trucks are operative for the season ahead

A Maine Summer Island: The Story of Bustins

Courtesy of Dean L. Lunt

Grandaughter Susie taking a walk on an idyllic summer day in 2007 along the island's only road.

Memorial Day Weekend and the first docking of the ferry with enthusiastic islanders of all ages

The island village reconvening; excited, high-decibel and hug-filled reunions

The annual Polar Bear Swim at Pidge's Cove for the young, the brave, the foolish

Chapter Three

Rusticators

SHORTLY after Portland became a city in 1832, ferry service began to carry locals to and from the Casco Bay islands. The first ferry, the *Kennebec*, bore little resemblance to the bumblebee black and yellow ferries of today's Casco Bay Lines that transport not only locals but hordes of tourists on scenic cruises of the bay.

In the years prior to the Civil War, little evidence existed to predict the arrival of a new subspecies, the tourist, in such numbers as to spearhead what one commentator has termed "the second discovery of the Maine coast." Nor would anyone have predicted that at the start of the twenty-first-century, tourism would be a major source of employment for Maine people and draw millions of out-of-state visitors.

The Civil War was not only a watershed event for our national political history, but also a watershed event for Maine both economically and socially.

The state's resource-oriented and labor-intensive economy was riding an ebbing tide. The day of the wooden commercial sailing vessel was passing. Maine granite would no longer be the material of choice for urban curbstones or buildings. The fishing industry was facing hard days, and the lobster canneries would close their doors. Food produced in the Midwest and transported east by the new railroads appeared on the shelves of Maine groceries at prices more than competitive with the prices of Maine-grown crops. The paper industry had yet to organize to exploit

Courtesy of Bustins Island Historical Society
Rusticators clamming on the shore in the early 1900s.

the vast tracts of Maine forest. In brief, Maine's economy found itself face-to-face with a huge void following the conclusion of the Civil War.

Into the void came tourism. Bustins Island was part and parcel of the change. The "second discovery of the Maine coast" can conveniently be assigned to the period after 1870. What Maine offered postwar America appeared to coincide neatly with what a number of citizens wanted and could afford. Maine's lack of development, its rural landscape and near-pristine coastline, along with improved rail transport to the state, seemed to offer an ideal answer to the national mania for outdoor life, the new concept of leisure time and vacation, and a freer spirit not embarrassed by a more conspicuous display of wealth and consumption. As a result of various promotional efforts from within the state, it became clear that Maine welcomed this new opportunity. Its scenic coastal vistas, good fishing, bracing water, and cool breezes awaited those summer migrants whom the *Bangor Industrial Journal* described as "professional and other over-worked and brain-wearied men from the large cities." By the end of the nineteenth century, according to one estimate, 300,000 tourists would be summering along the Maine coast.

Improved railroads helped open the way. Railroads and development went hand in hand. One fed the other. Owners of railroads encouraged development, and often built the hotels to which their rail lines brought guests. Amos Gerald of Fairfield was a major figure in these industries in the Freeport area. He was a principal in the electricity-generating plant that provided power for his Portland-to-Brunswick trolley line, which brought guests to the front doors of his Casco Castle hotel in South Freeport. The power plant and car barn were on the site of today's Public Safety Building in Freeport.

Development on Bustins began in 1892 on a much more modest scale than that also occurring in the Bar Harbor area at the same time. At the time, ownership of Bustins Island had essentially come to rest in the hands of the two families, the Swetts and the Merrills.

Henry Merrill, the Civil War veteran, had purchased his land, essentially half of the island, from Elisha Stover in 1876. Henry's brothers and his father took control of most of his holdings in 1883, although Henry continued to live on the island for some time.

Meanwhile, Benjamin Swett, who owned a meat business in Brunswick, and his wife, Amanda, first leased and then purchased most of the Horr property on August 31, 1891. The purchase excluded the land where the Horr sons had built their cottages, but included the Bibber farmhouse and nearby barn, as well as the northwest quarter of the island where the six-hole golf course would be built some years later. Amanda Swett was a sister to Mrs. Will Merrill.

These two families would spearhead the development of Bustins Island as a summer community. We know little about how the development plans came about, although, the August 10, 1911, edition of the *Casco Bay Breeze* referred to a conversation that probably took place in 1892: "While Captain [Horace] Townsend [of the ferry *Phantom*] and the Merrills were talking one day, they thought it would be a good scheme to boom Bustins Island as a place for summer homes for the people."

Apparently the Merrills, after reflecting on the development occurring along the coast and on other islands, and urged on by the entrepreneurial Townsend, decided to take advantage of the opportunity. They contracted Edwin C. Townsend, a prominent and very popular schoolteacher and variously town clerk, selectman, county commissioner, trial justice, and civil engineer, to

Courtesy of the Bustins Island Historical Society

Dancing outside The Berries in 1915.

survey their holdings on the island. He drew plans in 1892 and again in 1903. The 1946 Plot Plan of the island by Wallace L. Sawyer of Haverhill, Massachusetts (son of Nowell Sawyer who built the first summer cottage), notes that information was taken in part from plans of the Merrill holdings contained in plans of E. C. Townsend of Freeport. Perhaps it was Townsend as well who advised them to create postage-stamp sizes for many of the lots (66 by 100 feet), and to divide them into alphabetical sections A, B, C, and D, each with its own internal lot-numbering system. Perhaps they hoped to attract buyers with limited funds and some available summer time. This might include locals and, from away, teachers and preachers. The Merrill plan featured an area that ran along the shorefront designated as Shore Reserve. The Shore Reserve was to make sure all cottagers had access to the shore for recreational purposes. Soon the Merrills put their lots on the market.

The "booming" had begun.

The Swetts were quick to follow the Merrills in setting off lots near the water on both sides of the island. When H. N. Skolfield of Brunswick drew plans for Section E in 1921, he noted that they were based, with some changes, on plot plans by "Engineer Litchfield" of Brunswick in 1910 and other plans by T. P. Cutter in 1911. The Skolfield plan of 1921—along with the 1892, 1903 and 1912 Townsend plans of the Merrill holdings—would be combined in 1946 into Sawyer's Plot Plan. (However, it should be noted that the very first plans of the Swett lands were drawn not by Cutter or Litchfield, but by E. C. Townsend in 1896.)

They laid out a dozen or fifteen lots, some 60 by 100 feet and others 100 by 100 feet, on both sides of the island road. Later, when all of Section E was laid out, a different form of access to the shore was provided by establishing, at frequent intervals, rights-of-way from the island road. The intent of both sets of owners was to ensure that all islanders could reach the shoreline easily to picnic, swim, dig clams, and otherwise take advantage of what they had come to Bustins to enjoy—that world where sparkling sea meets ancient upthrust rock. Little thought was given to issues of where mean tide lines fell as regarded property rights or for the construction of docks for convenience's sake. These matters were inconsequential in comparison to the joyful reasons for which they had made the long and arduous pilgrimage to Maine and Bustins Island.

The first two summer cottages were built in 1892 and signaled the onset of the building boom with word of mouth serving as the primary method of advertising. Island View (currently owned by the Lahanas family) was built on the southeast side of the island by Nowell Sawyer of Bradford, Massachusetts. Sawyer had strong local connections. His wife was the daughter of Freeport's famed George Anderson, master builder of clipper ships. The Sawyers were also descendants of Jane Means, whose family is associated with the Means Massacre on Flying Point in 1756, when an Indian raiding party killed two family members, wounded another, and took captives. In any number of ways the Sawyers would have heard about the opportunity to buy and build on Bustins. Their arrival on the Freeport steamer *Phantom*, Captain Townsend at the wheel, was inauspicious by any standards.

"There was at that time just a temporary wharf on the southwest end of the island," they wrote, "about a hundred feet to the north of the present wharf. There wasn't a single house on the south side of the island when we arrived, just a rough cart road along the shore to the east. We had no sooner landed when it began to rain, thunder, and lightning something terrible."

The next year, 1893, the Merrill brothers, Josiah P. and William, joined with the operators of the Freeport Steamboat Company to build a more permanent wharf at the point of the island closest to South Freeport. This would facilitate the transport of

F. Benjamin Carr

Courtesy of the Bustins Island Historical Society
The steamboat Phantom *in the 1890s. Round-trip fare from Portland to South Freeport was 70 cents.*

freight, building materials, and passengers—who might be potential purchasers for their lots—to the island. Ten years later the Merrills sold the wharf to the Harpswell Steamboat Company. The sale included the land under the wharf to the low-water mark and the right to build a freight building and waiting room on the adjacent shore. In 1921, Casco Bay Lines, successor to the Harpswell Steamboat Company, sold the wharf to the Bustins Island Village Corporation with the same terms and with the stipulation that Casco Bay Lines would have the right to use the wharf free of all competition between June 25 and September 10 annually.

At the same time that the Merrills built the wharf in 1893, they employed Reuben Curtis, a carpenter formerly employed in the Freeport shipyards, to build cottages for their own use. Quinnebasset, long known as the Marr cottage and now owned by Fred and Betty Pease, was one of the cottages. The other, nearly adjacent, was Rocky Nook, later used by the Smoker family when they ran the summer store and restaurant in the 1940s, and now owned by Carol Dibrell. Curtis became the principal cottage builder on Bustins, building a cottage for himself as well as cottages for a number of other new rusticators before the century ended.

The Pidge and Kelsey cottages (owned today by Elaine Wilmot and Pat and Rob Gempel, respectively) were built in 1893, also on the Merrill property. One was built for *Phantom* skipper Horace Townsend and the other for John Kelsey of Freeport. The correspondent noting in June 1893 the start of construction on the Kelsey cottage, added: "We expect that within a few years this island will be one of the principal summer resorts in this part of the Bay."

In his 1960 Bustins history, George Richardson chronicles the rapid growth of cottages in the ensuing years. Nine cottages were built in 1894, some for prices in the $300- to $400-dollar range, on lots purchased from the Merrills for as little as $25. It did not take long for word to ripple through the Freeport community that these lots were for sale. Perhaps others heard about the opportunities in other ways. Tourists might have heard it from deckhands on the ferry from Portland; regular service to Chebeague Island had begun in 1875. Even more likely, they might have learned of the opportunities as they rode the *Phantom*, which stopped at Bustins as it hauled freight and passengers between Portland, Freeport, Mere Point, Birch Island, and Harpswell. It was aboard the *Phantom* that the Sawyers had first come to Bustins. Some renters reported having seen a notice of the cottage [Captain Townsend's Travelers Rest] in *Glimpses of Portland and Casco Bay, Maine*, the publicity piece published in Portland in the mid-1890s and directed toward tourists and land buyers. It praised Bustins for its "abundant supply of the purest water . . . pronounced to be equal to the celebrated Poland Spring water." Youthful guests at Will Merrill's Rocky Nook in 1894 were from Maine and Massachusetts and came with chaperones as was the custom of the day. The Bay Staters went home and, according to an August article in the *Six Town Times*, "they are to bring 100 strangers next year."

In May 1896, the *Six Town Times* reported that a Mr. Soule of Roxbury, Massachusetts, had purchased lot number four and planned to begin building immediately. The cottage would be the twenty-fifth one built on the island, nearly 25 percent of the total number of cottages on the island today.

In the same year, Benjamin Swett, for his own convenience and to enhance the value of his lots, built a wharf on the east side, just below the spot where a cottage would be built the next year for the Carberry family. That cottage, known today as The Berries, is owned by the Tozier family. Freight and passengers could be landed conveniently while a barrel hauled to the top of a flagpole—at either the Swett or Merrill wharves—signaled steamer captains to stop at the island.

Swett, meanwhile, continued to use the island as an adjunct to his Brunswick meat business. In July of 1897 he was reported to be "loading his [island] hay on his scow as fast as he cuts it and intends to scow it up to the head of Maquoit Bay and haul it from there to his home in Brunswick." He swam cows over from Flying Point, had a henhouse, grew a big garden each year with the help of a hired man, and did lots of fishing. According to his grandson, Charles Kitchin, Swett's reputation as a fisherman was such that people claimed he needed only to stand on his wharf and whistle whereupon the lobsters scurried to fill his traps.

With the number of cottages on the island rapidly growing, seasonal service businesses soon opened to serve the growing community. In May 1896 the *Six Town Times* carried news that J. W. Merrill planned to build a store and restaurant. The restaurant would seat thirty, "and so the weary housewives . . . may revel in our 'ideal Arcadie.'" The Ships Inn opened just before the Fourth of July. "It is a much-needed convenience and will make a great addition to the comfort of the transient as well as all summer visitors," said the newspaper on July 3. The following summer, trade was "so brisk that it seems necessary for the convenience of their patrons to keep [the restaurant] open 24 hours a day."

The store provided convenience for islanders and reopened annually into the 1970s, when its demise resulted from the combination of lower prices and greater variety in the handy supermarkets ashore. In addition, islanders increasingly owned powerboats, making it easy to go ashore for supplies. Early commodity prices defy belief: lobster was ten cents a pound, milk six cents a quart, tomatoes six cents a pound, and lettuce five cents a head.

The post office, in the same building as the store, bore the postal address "Seeket" given by Mrs. E. E. Pinkham who, with her husband, Freeport's postmaster, owned the west-side cottage built in 1893 that today belongs to the Rudolph family. It has been suggested that she chose the name because no one could/would decide whether the island was Bustins or Bibbers. In any event, with mail reaching the island twice daily by 1905, a confusing situation existed. Residents of Bustins Island discovered their island labeled Bibbers Island on navigational charts even as they received mail at their island postal address of Seeket, Maine. This confusion finally ended in 1908 when postal authorities approved a request to change the island address from Seeket to Bustins, and a year later when the Casco Bay Steamship Company listing changed from Bibbers to Bustins. Charts would be corrected only much later.

Access to the island had grown apace. Ferry service to Chebeague Island started about 1875. Some thirteen years later the 75-foot-long *Phantom*, built at South Freeport for the Freeport Steamboat Company, began to carry freight and passengers with stops in Freeport, Wolfe's Neck, Mere Point, Birch Island, Harpswell Lookout, Bustins, Chebeague, Littlejohn, Cousins, Falmouth Foreside, and Portland. *Phantom* made two trips daily to Portland, leaving at 6:45 a.m. and returning at 10:00 a.m. on her first circuit, and then leaving again at 2:00 p.m. and returning at 4:50 p.m. from her second circuit. The fare to Portland was seventy cents each way. Passengers could choose between a trip in the open air—and flying cinders—on the upper deck or a cleaner but stuffy journey on the lower deck. A bonus for passengers was the opportunity to watch cargo being loaded and unloaded using the derrick and boom on the ferry's foredeck. The Portland connection was significant because islanders often came on the overnight steamer from Boston to Portland where, with the two or three trunks full of necessities required for a summer's stay, they could take a ferry directly to Bustins.

By 1896, the *Phantom* was joined by the *Alice* on the run from Porter's Landing to Portland with Bustins as a stop. While schedules existed for all these ferries, they weren't always honored. For instance, a number of men, including Charles Dillingham and Will Merrill, spent a Labor Day on the island. When the ferry failed to arrive to return them to the mainland, they were forced to spend another night on the island before rowing ashore the next morning.

In 1898, a new dock was ready for the season. When the summer season opened, however, the *Phantom* was not running. The Spanish-American War may have been one factor; so was an unexplained obstruction in the bay that also prevented the *Madeleine* from running. Her owner hoped that within two or three weeks the obstruction would be removed and the steamer would be able to resume service between South Freeport, Porter's Landing, and Bustins. Meanwhile, it was proposed that E. A. Baker of Portland lease his steam launch, capacity thirty, to carry people. Shortly after mid-month, however, normal services resumed. "Didn't it seem good," the *Six Town Times* reported on July 22, "to hear that prolonged whistle and screech of the steamer, 'all aboard for Bustins,' last Tuesday morning? Those wretched Spaniards came near cheating us out of the privilege for the summer."

By summer's peak seven boats per day were touching Bustins, including the *Madeleine*, the *Tremont*, and the *Corinna*.

Over the next years a variety of cottage rentals became available. In 1904, the builder Reuben Curtis offered a new six-room cottage for $35 per month. Two small two-room cottages were offered at $15 and $25 for the season. Mary Ellen Patterson, the *Casco Bay Breeze* reporter on Bustins in 1904, rented rooms in her Waumbek cottage (today's Larrabee cottage) for $1 per day and up, including board. Restaurant manager Herbert Dillingham provided board at the Ships Inn for $5 per week. Still, demand

Courtesy of the Bustins Island Historical Society

The steamer Tourist.

exceeded supply. With no hotel as yet, "would-be visitors have sought accommodation in vain," wrote the *Casco Bay Breeze*. Soon an effort was made to remedy this deficiency. In 1907 the first—and only—Bustins hotel, the Casco Queen, was built behind the present LaFleur cottage for George Lavers of Freeport. Lavers also operated the island bakery (present Lahanas cottage) and used the LaFleur cottage as a hotel annex. In 1910, the hotel had twenty-one guests including Dr. and Mrs. Eugene Eugster and Mr. and Mrs. Walter Hunziker. Both couples were so taken with the island that they quickly bought land and had their own cottages built. The hotel burned in 1914.

Boating also played a role on Bustins Island. At an early date Will Soule sailed the *Argonauta*, John Kelsey the *Xanadu*, and S. T. Merrill the *Eldina* (built by Josiah Merrill in 1895). The starter touched off the first yacht race on July 27, 1897, with races scheduled for succeeding Saturdays through August. Spectators were reminded that they could take the noon boat from Porter's Landing and return on the 6:45 so as to be home in good season. Between seven and ten boats raced each Saturday, following a course chosen to take advantage of prevailing summer breezes. From a starting point between Bustins and Little Bustins, the contestants sailed southwestward to the Green Island ledge marker and then on an easterly course to the marker off Goose Ledge (between Lower Goose and Little Whaleboat islands) and then home. By the middle of the following summer a movement was afoot to start a yacht club. A committee was appointed to draw up a constitution and prepare a list of officers to be presented for approval prior to the next week's race. A fifty-cent entrance fee was to be charged for each boat entered, and a silver cup was to be awarded to the winner of two out of the three races. As many as two hundred spectators gathered to watch the races.

Before long, boats with gasoline engines began making inroads. In 1904, an article in the *Casco Bay Breeze* noted that John Ray, who owned The Port cottage, was finally reconciled to the "steady use of gasoline in his small boat instead of white ash." In 1907, fifteen powerboats raced over a 7-mile course with Charles Guppy the winner in forty-nine minutes.

Early rusticators on Bustins established routines that they expected to follow daily. Dr. Marr went to the store each day, and the tale is told of his once catching a twist of the store's big spool of twine around his foot. As he walked homeward up the hill, the spool in the store jerked each time he put his right foot forward. Dr. Eugster took his meals at the restaurant, and each evening after supper he would stride up the hill, trailing smoke from a freshly lit cigar. His wife, Alice, walked several paces behind. Mr. Miller had a little pony cart that pulled him around the island.

A weekly worship service, usually taking advantage of any clergyman staying on-island, took place at one time in the grove near where the public float is found today. Later, until the Community House was built in 1920, services were held on land where Roger Leland's generator house now stands. A little shelter was built there with a raised platform for the preacher and space to store the pump organ and some chairs. The Bustins Island Athletic Association purchased copies of the *Chapel Hymnal* for use at the services.

Other events also took place in the grove. In 1905, Dick Sugatt's Refined Vaudeville Company played on the island. In August 1910, *The Elopement of Ellen* was staged in the grove, starring islander Elizabeth MacDonald and an all-female cast.

The correspondent for the *Six Town Times* regaled the paper's readers with accounts of the island's social events, including whist evenings (Military or Dutch), peanut hunts for the children, and candy-pulling contests. The island ladies gathered to do handwork, including embroidery, drawn and Mexican work, and Battenburg lace.

Music was big. The center of attraction at the Pinkham cottage in 1898 was "a sweet-toned gramophone." At another gala, Mrs. Filman delighted the guests with her ragtime cakewalk; in fact, dancing to the strains of ragtime music—the "Georgia Camp Meeting" was a favorite—was all the rage one summer.

The islanders went to great lengths with their parties, decorating with buntings, evergreens, and Chinese lanterns. They dressed up frequently and for all sorts of events, from luncheons at the store to afternoon tea parties to meeting the ferry.

Charles Guppy, who, with his wife Margaret, had come to Bustins about 1885 and built his own cottage in 1886, often took islanders on moonlight cruises with serenading an integral part of the evening.

In the new century baseball games were played against teams from Freeport, Birch Island, and elsewhere. Trips were taken to such places as Merrymeeting Park, Peaks Island Theatre, the Elijah Kellogg Church on Harpswell, and Mere Point for a dance. Clambakes were a social high point, as was a dinner honoring Captain Mayo of the sloop *Iris* who generously took many islanders out for afternoon sails.

In 1906, the social calendar included berry picking on neighboring French's Island, a trip to the Casco Castle hotel in South Freeport, and games of the day, including Pit and Jenkins. The next year it was reported in the *Casco Bay Breeze* that "the golf grounds and tennis courts are getting into good condition."

The Bustins Island Athletic Association handled many issues pertaining to island "sojourners" during the early years. But in

Ken Wilson Collection, Bustins Island Historical Society
The ferry Spindrift *with Dick Taisey at the wheel.*

1904, the association's executive committee proposed creating an association to manage island issues and finances. So was born the Bustins Island Cottagers Association. The first meeting was held in the grove on the afternoon of July 17, 1905. Minutes of the association, predecessor to the Bustins Island Village Corporation, are illuminating. The association dealt with issues ranging from garbage collection to tennis courts to lighting to gypsy moth destruction to the road conditions, which was an annual issue then as now.

    The association continued even after the village corporation was formed in 1913. It sponsored the annual Bustins Bust talent show, which was used to raise money for various causes. For example, in 1919, $50 was sent to the Red Cross for French war orphans. Money raised was also used to purchase a piano and build a new tennis court. And the minutes for August 21, 1923, note the "rumor that South Freeport visitors are coming to Island dances. Committee will consider." Today the Cottagers Association of Bustins Island (CABI), as it is now known, remains a vital force in the island community.

F. Benjamin Carr

Prior to the building of the Community House in 1920, many of the communal social activities took place in the dining room of the store. In the 1990 winter-spring newsletter of the Bustins Island Historical Society, islander Nicki Kitchin provided a bird's-eye view of some of these activities in 1916, when the season was ushered in with a series of dances in the dining room—modern dances, Virginia reels, Paul Joneses, and the Boston Fancy—all performed to Victrola music. Admission was 15 cents, or 25 cents a couple. There were "serving parties," too, where Mrs. Cole served raspberry sundaes and fancy cakes. Card games were played here as well.

Groups from off-island contributed to the social mix. Sunday School picnics were regularly held on the island with students coming from Freeport by ferry. In 1897, the Freeport High

Collection of Edmund P. Skillin, Freeport Historical Society
The old store prior to the addition of the Ships Inn restaurant, c. 1896.

School class of 1887 held its ten-year reunion on Bustins. On Labor Day of the same year the Freeport Masons sponsored a mammoth clambake on the island, preceded by a baseball game and followed by a yacht race. The Brunswick High School girls' basketball team stayed at Sunset cottage (now Koleda's) in 1904.

A number of islanders brought with them a love of golf.

"On Thursday July 12 [1900]," according to an article in the *Six Town Times*, "an enthusiastic group of young people met at the cottage Adneda to form a golf club. It was ascertained that through the kindness of Mr. Swett and Mr. Merrill the links could be located in their fields at the eastern end of the island . . . the club will start with a membership of 15 or 20."

That same summer twenty vacationers vied in the island's first tournament. Miss Greuel led the ladies with a score of 77, while W. W. Curtis's 57 was good enough to hold off his male rivals. Over the next years golf played a significant role in helping islanders enjoy their island sojourn. Frank Garfield told of the eager golfers who, before the east-side had so many cottages, established holes along the east side roads with the result that the golfers "played" their way through three holes before they reached the six-hole course itself. Eventually interest waned and the course fell into disuse through the later decades of the century. But with the enthusiasm and hard work of the Kirkland family, the encroaching puckerbrush was cut back, the original holes rediscovered, and the course restored for use by islanders of all ages and their guests.

Sportfishing in the waters off Bustins was a pastime embraced by many of the men. In the early years it was inextricably bound with the Horrs who had remained on the island even as the summer people began to arrive and build, and who were still angling regularly—not always for fish. In 1896 Will Horr lassoed a deer swimming off Williams Island and brought it to Bustins from which it soon swam away. More typically he provided what was in fact an early party boat, taking groups to the fishing grounds he knew so well. One group he took in 1897 came back with over 400 pounds of fish. On another occasion he caught an 8-and-a-half-foot shark, weighing around 600 pounds, in his pogie net. Will's brother Jake also fished; in June of 1899 he "captured from dragging 68 mackerel recently, the combined weight of which was 101 pounds," according to the *Six Town Times*. Jake was married on Bustins; his was the first wedding on the island in a long time, perhaps ever. Almost immediately, however, he and his new bride moved to Long Island, closer to Portland. Lots of private fishing occurred as well. In 1897 Josiah Merrill, by then eighty-six, went out and caught fifteen large mackerel. And on the commercial level, Charles Guppy reportedly caught 1,200 pounds of smelt on one tide in December. These he sold ashore to help earn enough money to get his family through the long winter ahead.

"Gunning" for sea ducks was the third way men spent their time. This occurred primarily off-season in the fall and spring, outside the customary rusticating months. Dr. Twitchell of Portland and Mr. Pinkham of Freeport were inveterate gunners. In September 1897 they "secured a nice bag of over 40 birds," according to the *Six Town Times*. A year later the correspondent for the newspaper related that "throughout the past week there [has] been almost one continuous echo of rifles and guns, while the sportsmen returned each evening with no end of game." Coot, black duck, sheldrake, and whistler were the primary varieties available to the hunters.

Clearly entertainment was not in short supply. Latter-day cottagers have developed through the CABI an extensive program of social activities with events scheduled every weekend and often during the week. These activities range from boat parades to poster contests, from bake sales to pancake breakfasts to the traditional Fourth of July ham and bean supper in the Community House. Square dances are sponsored for the young of all ages, as well as story hours, a youth and an adult library, and a Fourth of July parade followed by a hot dog lunch. The Annual Field Day at the golf course, featuring three-legged races, egg-passing relay races, and other events requiring skill and teamwork as well as speed, is an eagerly awaited event.

Bustins residents, who now hail from all over the country, appear to have become increasingly protective of their island as time has passed. Consternation is expressed on those rare occasions when the island is mentioned in the *Maine Sunday Telegram's* "Vacationland Guide." Delicate suggestions have often been made to our ferry captains that they should not bring the curious to the island. This is a sticky wicket at best. We are not being fair to our ferrymen—who depend on passengers for their income, and for whom the season is painfully brief—if we expect them to stand beside their boat where half a dozen passengers are loading luggage and say, "Sorry, I'm too full," or "Not this trip, perhaps another day."

Some years ago prolonged debate between islanders concerned construction of an outhouse for public use—complementing the one in the bushes adjacent to the Community House in the interior of the island. One faction argued that "a public outhouse will send the message that it's OK to come and visit Bustins; if we don't have one, 'they' won't come." The opposing faction argued, more realistically, that "if 'they' don't find facilities, 'they' will use the puckerbrush. Besides, we need facilities for our own children using the swings or playing basketball or

Courtesy of Dean L. Lunt
Henry Kirkland mowing the island's six-hole golf course in 2007.

volleyball." Only following several years of discussion was the outhouse built and promptly tucked away in the bushes where only the informed could find it. A card tacked to the wall inside advises users to see the postmistress if no toilet paper is available. Postmistress Olive is 100 yards away in her office that is open a few hours a day in July and August.

In 1995, an article in the *Boston Sunday Globe* highlighting Bustins shattered our sense of insularity and presented us with the apparition of day-trippers overrunning the island. Miriam Butts, ever cognizant of island sentiments and possessed of a delightful sense of humor, suggested in the Bustins Island Historical Society newsletter that one option to meet the potential incursion of day-trippers was to share Bustins, but to treat it like a national park, and limit the times and dates of such happenings, e.g., once in a thousand years. Her suggestion evoked laughter—and agreement! After talking with a reporter from the Portland paper, Kip Shields explained apologetically, "I didn't want to paint the island up too much; we don't want visitors."

To attribute all these feelings to protectionism is to highlight the seamy side of the problem. For a problem it is. All cottage owners pay taxes to the Town of Freeport. A percentage of that tax money is returned to Bustins to be used in support of all kinds of budgeted projects, not least of which is road maintenance. Roads maintained with public monies cannot be labeled private roads; they are available for public use. How to acknowledge the truth of this basic fact while at the same time preserving our privacy presents a vexing problem for us, one that has not been solved in any final way. But to say that Bustins folk are snobbish—"Palm Beach North" as we were once labeled by a Freeport official with an image of the island as a stronghold of the wealthy—needs to be tempered by what is closer to the fact. Bustins, to its ferociously loyal and committed residents, is a refuge, a little backwater of God, a special spot to be protected at all costs.

We can sit on the bench by the Public Dock and look straight up the bay into Portland, see the tankers at anchor as they await the chance to unload at the Merrill or Irving docks in South Portland, pick out the looming shape of the large condominium building on the Eastern Promenade, and shake our heads over the thin gray-brown haze that hangs over the city on a windless day. Simultaneously we feel gratitude that we can be on an island that to most seems a century or more removed from the bustle and growth, the world-with-us of Portland and the mainland. Our protectiveness for Bustins has everything to do with wanting to preserve a refuge, a place where we know and are known, a precious place to go when we become world-weary. A century and a half after they first discovered Maine, we maintain the tradition pioneered by the rusticators.

Chapter Four

Ralph, Lilly and Archie

THREE Mainers who played critical roles on Bustins over the last half century were Ralph and Lilly Brewer and Archie Ross.

Ralph Brewer

Ralph Brewer, born in 1900, usually wore a ragged old cap, a blue shirt unbuttoned to the waist, a greasy T-shirt, and huge rubber wader boots folded down at the top. His pants usually sagged beneath his oversized belly. Sometimes he drove an old Chevy pickup without doors (later bought for $5 and still used today with the same set of tires by Fred Pease). Ralph's family on his father's side had lived in the Freeport area since 1753. He settled on the island in the 1930s, but had come earlier with his father to work in Laver's bakery, to serve ice cream at the Casco Queen hotel, and to build the Barrows cottage, among others. He also worked as a dynamiter at a feldspar mine in Minot (source of a lovely collection of tourmalines he stored in a cigar box), a lumberjack, and a caulker in a local shipyard. Of course, like many of his era he was a farmer, fisherman, builder of barns and piers, and an all around handyman. Allegedly, Ralph even tried his hand at rum-running when his father was dying and money was desperately needed for medicine. During his Bustins years he still owned an old lobster boat, the *Sinbad*, that he pulled out for the winter over by the golf course.

Ralph was the island superintendent, living with his wife during the season in the Brewer cottage. His job description—never written or carefully defined—guaranteed variety. The island dock needed to be launched in the spring, maintained during the summer, and hauled at year's end. The dirt and gravel roads required constant maintenance. The old fire truck and island tractor always needed tinkering. Ralph mowed the golf course, hauled and delivered kerosene for stoves and lamps, and fixed cottages' pitcher pumps. Behind his own cottage in the middle of the island lay his barn, a mind-boggling storehouse of hard-to-find pump parts, one-of-a-kind tools, and a variety of other treasures.

As superintendent/caretaker he visited the island when possible during the winter, crossing the ice from Flying Point, to see whether the winds and ravages of winter had blown open any cottage doors or caused other damage. Ralph beefed up his meager official stipend by doing all sorts of odd jobs for islanders. He opened and closed cottages, cut grass, installed septic systems and cleaned outhouses, built and repaired docks, reshingled cottage roofs, hauled skiffs at season's end, and generally—very much on his own timetable and in his own fashion—provided whatever services islanders might request.

The ice business was still going strong during Ralph's early years on the island. In the spring, Ralph cut ice from the ponds and stored it in the adjacent icehouses to deliver when summer finally returned. Ralph delivered ice in a wagon drawn by an old and tired brown horse named Johnson. When Ralph took out his ice pick to cut down a block to icebox size, the ever-present island young would grab the flying chips to cool their throats. Ken Roberts remembers that Ralph would drop in if he saw Ken's dad, Don, in the kitchen when he was delivering ice at 7:00 in the morning. After they talked a couple minutes, Don would ask Ralph if he would like a "little something." Ralph would hold up three fingers horizontally, and add "with a little

F. Benjamin Carr

Courtesy of Olive Nickerson

Ralph Brewer in the 1950s.

chaser." Since Ralph was missing most of one finger on one hand, this really meant "four fingers." Ken's dad would get out two glasses and put about two inches of bourbon in one and fill the other with water. Ralph would down the bourbon, say "Thank you very much," and get back to delivering ice. "In all the years I witnessed this," Ken said, "I never once saw Ralph touch the water."

About mid-century bottled gas gradually replaced ice and kerosene as the fuel of choice for refrigerators, stoves, hot water heaters, and lighting. After ice was cut for the last time, about 1953, Ralph went into the bottled gas business through Rings of Yarmouth. He also maintained the equipment that used the gas.

A Maine Summer Island: The Story of Bustins

His visits were always colorful. Sometimes Ralph could be enticed to do a needed job with the promise of fresh-baked cookies, but usually something stronger was needed. One islander was anxious for Ralph's assistance in adjusting the thermostat on a new stove, but couldn't get Ralph to help. Ralph offered many excuses. Finally the islander hit the right note. "I just bought a six-pack back from the mainland; have you got time for a cold one?" Quicker than it takes to tell the tale, Ralph huffed and puffed his way up to the cottage, downed one "to steady my nerves," and somehow found time to adjust the thermostat before Lilly caught up with him.

Ralph never minced words. Shortly after Fred Pease moved into the old cottage he had recently bought, he asked Ralph where on the property the septic system had been situated.

"When you have to know, you'll know," Ralph answered.

Another islander stopped Ralph on the road and asked about reshingling his cottage roof.

"That'd be $600," Ralph answered with barely a pause.

"That seems a lot of money," the cottager responded.

"Well, you got two choices . . . take it or leave it."

A female islander sent a message that she wanted to see him, and Ralph obliged. "You know I went over there—I guess it was kinda early in the morning," Ralph said. "She leaned out her upper winder and hollered to me. She had a pair of bags like a new milk cow hanging right out over the windersill."

Occasionally, Ralph could be convinced to attend a potluck supper. One supper included the Gateses, Whitings, MacDonalds, and others. Jean Whiting was responsible for hors d'oeuvres and a shrimp dish, very Chinese and very ornate. Ralph took one bite.

"If that's what you call supper," he said, "I guess I'll go home."

And out he went, the screen door banging behind him.

Ralph took on young islanders for summer work that often included caring for the grass growing around one cottage or another. Ralph always said there were no lawns on Bustins—only grass. The first day on the job included an introduction to his tired gas rotary push mower. After minimal instruction in starting and using the machine, he said, "When you're done, push this metal strip into the spark plug to shut down the motor, and then turn it on its side."

"Why do I have to turn it on its side?" he was asked.

"This little valve here is broke. If you don't turn it on its side, all the gas will leak out."

"Why don't you just replace the valve?"

"New valve costs a dollar. Turnin' her on her side costs nothin'."

A less appealing part of his work included dealing with the vagaries of island septic systems. The old Wade cottage, the Universal Joint, had a cast-iron sewer line which extended straight down from the second floor of the cottage, past the Toziers, to the bay. Two final sections reached the low-water mark. John

Collection of Freeport Historical Society

Ralph's boatyard.

Jaynes unclogged the last two sections annually. One year the pipes backed up all the way to the second floor. John decided that the obstruction was close to the shore. He had his big wrench, some 2x4s, and two helpers, his employee Guy Curit and Ralph. John wielded the wrench; the two others were positioned below, each with a piece of wood, to hold up the pipes. After the third bolt was loosened, the pipe began to leak. Ralph and Guy ducked a little, tightening the top bolt. "Raise up, there," called John. They straightened, the fourth bolt came off, the trickle increased. John rammed a long rod up the pipe and immediately waste cascaded out and down in a 6-foot-wide flare. John ducked and ran. The two men below, pipes on their shoulders, were trapped. John reconnected the pipes; Ralph and Guy headed out into the bay. Ralph never again dealt with those pipes.

One night Ralph fell through a stair in his cottage as he made his way up to bed. He fell backwards, wedging his leg tightly. Somehow Lilly—100 pounds—got Ralph—200-plus pounds—out of the broken stair and downstairs into a chair. "Can you get me a glass of water," he gasped, ashen-faced.

"My Gawd, I think he's dying," Lilly remembered thinking.

She called South Freeport on the CB just as Ralph lapsed into an unconsciousness that lasted until they got him ashore. The town ambulance was busy elsewhere that night and the backup, a hearse, was called into service. Ralph regained consciousness just as he was being loaded in. Realizing what kind of vehicle he was in, he yelled and screamed.

"At least I knew he was alive," Lilly reported later.

Ralph kept a hodgepodge of derelict boats up by the present barge landing beside the dump in what was known as Ralph's boatyard. Amongst them was his *Sinbad*. Marilyn, to be my wife one day, painted a watercolor of the *Sinbad* back in the early '50s. When Ralph saw it, he asked her what she would charge for it. "Twenty-five dollars," she told him.

"Hell," he retorted, "the whole damn boat ain't worth that much."

Ralph worked without the power equipment that makes work easier today. Brawn, determination, and old-fashioned skills were all ingredients of a successful venture into construction. Ken Roberts tells of one such venture that Ralph undertook.

"In the early fifties a group of south-shore cottagers got together to form Brainard's Landing Inc. They were, as I remember, Jeff Drew, Stu MacDonald, Bud Nickerson, Chet Deering, Don Roberts, and Helen Walton. Bud was president and Jeff was treasurer. All the members put up some money and contracted with Ralph to replace the Brainard's Landing cribs, which had become derelict, and build a new runway and float. There may have been an actual contract with Ralph, but I doubt it, since

Courtesy of Frank Garfield

Ralph Brewer standing at far left beside Marjorie Garfield in the 1960s. Walter Gardner stands at the far right. The two young men in the middle are Archie Ross and son Wayne Ross.

Ralph didn't much like paperwork. There may or may not have been a cost estimate.

"This was about the time that Eddie Legasse was building a new runway for George Richardson. He was using concrete for the piers, and the Brainard's Landing members suggested to Ralph that this might be the best way to go. Ralph gave them a dissertation on the fact that Legasse and his crew might be good carpenters in Massachusetts, but they knew nothing about building docks, especially docks on the coast of Maine. Concrete piers give a big area of resistance to the waves, which will eventually undermine them and wash them away. Richardson's dock probably won't last five years. [Ralph most likely did not use the modifier "probably," as he was prone to definite statements.] What was needed for Brainard's Landing, he said, were old-fashioned cribs, weighted with stones. The members decided to go with oak.

"Work began the next winter as Ralph ordered green oak logs, cut on two sides to 12-inch thickness, and delivered to Flying Point. He explained that green wood was essential, as sea worms do not like it. [This later turned out to be not totally true.] In the spring [of 1954] we destroyed the old cribs with sledgehammers and piled the stones that had been used for ballast onto a couple of WWII balsa life rafts that were then anchored offshore. Heaving around barnacle-encrusted boulders was not a lot of fun.

"We then floated the logs over to Bustins by towing them with 5-horsepower outboards on skiffs. Slow. The green lumber floated just below the surface, making the going tough. Those were the days when there were no power tools on Bustins. Power on this job consisted of manpower, the tide and a deadman 20-foot pole rigged vertically, at a slight slant with a pulley at the top and a line for hoisting by hand. Logs were floated, just barely, into position and tied in place while a worker drilled a three-quarter-inch hole at each end, into the log beneath, with a hand auger. Then he drove a 1-inch spike 24 inches long into each hole with a sledgehammer. A platform was built every 6 feet of height and rocks off-loaded from the life rafts onto the platforms to hold the crib in place. It must have taken five men and a boy (me) eight weeks to construct two cribs. Ralph was a great practical engineer. There were no drawings. Measurements, such as they were, were made with a tape measure and a carpenter's level.

"After the cribs were done, we built the runway. Because Ralph hated 'sidewalk superintendents,' we started on the sea side and worked toward land. Here again, Ralph's engineering skills came into play. He had us construct A-frames between the two cribs and between the inner crib and the shore. The tops of the A-frames were 2 feet higher than the headers on the cribs. We then put the stringers for the runway in place, cross-braced them and added stanchions and railings. The runway sections thus had 2-foot humps in the middle of them, but when we knocked away the A-frames, they dropped down to perfectly level, and because they were now in compression, they were extremely stable and strong.

"Before we had a chance to fully secure the runway to the cribs, Hurricane Carol came to Bustins and washed the runway onto the rocks in front of the Roberts cottage. The cribs (showing little resistance to the wind and waves) held firm. With a great deal of effort, a very high tide and a lot of swearing, Ralph and his crew got the runway off the rocks and back into place. It had sustained remarkably little damage.

"When the job was finally complete, the sidewalk superintendents noticed there was a slight bend in the runway where it crossed the innermost crib. Ralph maintained that was just the way he'd planned it.

"The Brainard's Landing you see today, with some repairs to the cribs to replace worm-eaten logs, and some new runway decking, is the same runway built by Ralph and his crew, by hand, nearly fifty years ago."

Ralph died of emphysema in 1968. Too many Camel cigarettes, as one longtime islander put it. He was sixty-eight. A resolution of tribute, written by Robert Dennett, was presented at that year's Annual Meeting in August. After offering condolences to his widow and the family, it noted that Ralph had a close and abiding relationship with Bustins Island for fifty-eight years and that gradually, over those years, Bustinites had become dependent upon Ralph and his many skills. Many of these skills were enumerated. It was also noted he "was always Ralph in a very special way to us all—youngster and oldster alike."

The words rang true.

Lilly Brewer

Lilly Brewer, born in 1906, came to Bustins Island in the 1940s. After a few years, she and Ralph shed their respective spouses and married one another. Lilly came from a family of clammers whose habit had been to move on before the next rent was due. Over the years Lilly had led a colorful life, including a stint as cook in a lumber camp. She had five children, two of whom, Maxine and Burt, are remembered fondly by older islanders. She was redheaded, resourceful, warm, and full of zest, with an ever-ready laugh and a salty tongue. Harriet Garfield recalled that Lilly taught her "the mechanics of how to keep house on Bustins: how to wash lamp chimneys, keep oil in the receptacles, watch out for flare-ups."

On the island Lilly's primary transport was an old bicycle. A whistle always announced her arrival at a cottage door—and her arrival was always welcome. Ashore she owned a succession of cars. I most vividly remember a much-used orange Plymouth Barracuda. One winter evening I came home from school—I was teaching then at Mt. Holyoke—to find her Plymouth outside and Lilly, with an ear-to-ear grin, waiting. She had offered no hint that she would be arriving; she just assumed that I'd be home sometime. We had a lovely visit, full of gossip and yarns; the candles burned late. Right after breakfast the next morning, Lilly climbed back into her hatchback and off she headed for her next port of call.

Like Ralph, she undertook any needed odd job. Opening cottages and getting them aired out and ready for summer was a specialty. She removed storm panels from doors, puttied a window or two, put up the screens, dusted and swept, hung curtains, made beds, and cleaned out any mouse nests. Hardly any cottages were available for rent then, but Lilly always knew who might rent a cottage for a week or two. A letter to her would elicit a prompt and warm response saying that she thought the Eugster cottage might be available, or that Ken Bancroft might be willing to rent his cottage for an off-season week.

She was also a practical joker. Reportedly she attached bells under Roger Leland's bed before he arrived on island for his honeymoon. She also persuaded Donny Ulrickson to lay plate glass over the top of Joe Johnson's chimney so that when the fire was lit, his cottage filled with smoke—even if he had taken the precaution of looking up the chimney first to be sure it was uncovered.

Lilly was a good cook—not just for a gang of hungry lumberjacks in camp but also for islanders. Jean Whiting remembers that once a year Lilly prepared traditionally baked haddock with cream sauce and hard-boiled eggs for a group of west-siders. She was also noted for shore dinners—clams, lobsters, and all the fixings actually prepared on the shore, and for her sweet pink and white peppermint patties, snapped up immediately by those in the know at cake sales.

After Ralph's death Lilly became the island superintendent. The worst part of the job, to her thinking, was the Annual Report she needed to present at the Annual Meeting. Pencil-written in longhand on large sheets from a pad, her report presented a view of the island comprehensible to every last islander

Lilly Brewer, 1966. Courtesy of Olive Nickerson

and written by a friend who loved the island. Eventually Lilly learned to avoid the dreaded meetings; her apologetic request to be excused, submitted in writing each year, came to be expected and received with laughter. No one questioned that each year on the first Saturday in August, some crisis would befall Lilly that necessitated her being off the island. She would hotfoot it down her woods path to the cove by the dump where she kept her skiff and abandon the island.

When she first took the job, however, she stood up and delivered her report. "Well, it is about that time again, and I am told I must have a report ready. I am no good at making reports, but I'll try." She reported on the roads, bushes "that like to slap you as you went by" and which she had clipped once already, the trucks that needed plugs or other attention, the public wells that passed inspection, except for the Community House where "the kids put soap in it." She noted that "of course, someone had to take the fire truck out. It seems someone does every year. Either the 4th or Labor Day." (She had eyes in the back of her head; she always knew which young people had taken the truck joyriding. They loved her because, as son Burt relates, she could "chew ass one day and be best of friends the next.") On a different subject, she informed meeting attendees that "the red tide has not bothered us much yet so we still have good clamming." Finally, with evident relief, she reached her conclusion. "Guess that's all I can think of right now. Hope the weather will be good and you all have a very nice vacation." A few desultory questions might be asked and then the meeting settled back for the next item on the agenda.

Often, while cottagers gathered on one porch or another in the evening to recount the day's events and share a few drinks and nibbles, Lilly would pedal by and be hailed and invited to come up and sit. Midge Walker remembers one such time when she was enjoying crackers with some Liederkranz cheese.

When Midge passed Lilly an hors d'oeuvre, Lilly's succinct one-word comment was "Gawd."

"Don't you like it, Lilly?" Midge asked.

"Don't know," Lilly replied. "Never ate it, but I stepped in it plenty of times back on the farm."

A Maine Summer Island: The Story of Bustins

Lilly had another side that surfaced in her poetry. She was untrained, but her poems, written for her own pleasure, are perceptive and rise directly from the heart. They deal with her world, frequently the natural world around her seen in seasons when most of us were far away from Maine. In 1977, when Lilly died of pneumonia (cancer treatments had wiped out her immune system) at age seventy, a poem that islanders especially loved was read at her funeral. A framed copy hangs aboard the island ferry, the *Lilly B.*, named in her honor.

Beautiful Bustins Island

Have you ever been on Bustins in winter?
It's a wonderful sight to behold.
Everything covered with ice and snow
Beautiful clean and cold.
Some think it desolate and dreary
But, on a nice clear winter's day
You lose all your cares and troubles
As you look out over the Bay.
The rippling waves are frozen
The shores are covered with ice
To me it can never be dreary
For me there's no place as nice.
There are no boats at anchor
No white sails against the sky
No soft thick fog to engulf you
No scream of the gulls as they fly.
As you follow the paths, 'tis so pretty
The trees are all covered with snow
There isn't a sound to be heard
Not even the call of a crow.
The houses are cold and shuttered

F. Benjamin Carr

There is quietness everywhere
No smoke from the chimneys rising
To drift lazily thru' the air.
There is no sound of an outboard
No bark of a dog to be heard
For here on the island in winter
Noise—is only a word.

Archie Ross

Archie Ross, son of Eli and Mary (Marie) Ross of Chebeague Island, was born in March of 1924. His sister Lavinia helped raise him; he in turn helped support the family by clamming with his father. He became a whistler and a whittler, skills that would stay with him throughout his life. That he would be a seafarer seemed almost inevitable. "My father and grandfather on both sides worked on the water," he told *The Forecaster* newspaper in 1996. "My grandfathers were captains, and my father was a fisherman who made a living doing what they called 'vessel fishing'—with a net, and from a dory—and lobstering, clamming, all sorts of things."

It was no wonder that the ledges became his old acquaintances, the sea breezes his close friends, the tides his daily companions. His first job was as deckhand on the *Nellie G.*, converted from steam to gas, which ran from Handy Boat in Falmouth Foreside to Cousins, Littlejohn, and Chebeague islands.

Archie was ineligible for the military during World War II; at 90 pounds, he did not meet the minimum weight requirement of 105 pounds. Instead he taught seamanship and boat handling to navy personnel and ran boats to and between the military installations in Casco Bay. Later he returned to service on the *Nellie G.*, the *Nellie G. III*, and the *Victory*, all owned by the Swett family of Falmouth and offering service to the islands of the bay. In the off-season he supported himself as a merchant mariner and by service aboard the Portland pilot boat. He also built boats—forty or more; "I don't dare to guess exactly how many"—as a half-partner, with Carroll Lowell, at the Even Keel Boatyard in Yarmouth.

In 1946, the Bustins ferry run was open. The previous summer had marked the last year of long-running ferry services provided by John Jaynes and the Guppys. John decided to captain the *Peg*, a boat belonging to and used by the Barnards to whom he was related through his wife. Al Guppy perhaps felt his boat no longer met the standards of the islanders. Libby Silver tells the story of how, in the Guppys' last summer of 1945, her sister Mary was pregnant and on Bustins when she nearly had a miscarriage. Mary liked to tell how she was taken—on a door as a stretcher—to the mainland on Al Guppy's boat. It was pouring rain. His old boat was open at both ends. Most of her body was under the canvas cover, but her head was sticking out. Some man who was standing in the open and collecting rain on his sou'wester hat would bend over now and then to ask her if she was all right and dump the water in her face. The story ended happily some months later when Mary's daughter Carol was born.

The Swetts took over the island run in 1946, using the *Victory*. Archie was a twenty-two-year-old crew member and owned no boat of his own when, at season's end, the island's Board of Overseers offered him the job of providing ferry service to Bustins the next year. He accepted and immediately bought the *Victory* from the Swetts. His service to the island would span fifty years. The next May he received a typed legal contract, and though uncomfortable with such a formal approach, Archie signed. He was guaranteed $15 per day off-season (June 15–25) and $20 per day in-season (June 25–September 15). The contract, signed by Homer Weston, William Obear, Dana Norris, and George Ramsdell, stipulated that if gross receipts from mail contracts, freight, and passengers exceeded these figures, the

Village Corporation owed Archie nothing. Otherwise he would be paid the difference at season's end.

From the very beginning he was a smashing success, quickly winning a warm place in the hearts of every islander. For fifty years he would be an integral part of island life and island families. Passengers felt they were already on Bustins as soon as they took a seat on the boat. It was said that babies learned to say "Archie" before they learned to say "Daddy." Young women expressed their feelings for him in verse.

On the first run of the year he would grin at the expectant islanders. "Let's see if I remember how to run this boat." Later in the season, members of each returning family would be greeted warmly. "I'm awful glad to see you again. I really am."

At 5:15 in the afternoon, waiting with a boatful of impatient passengers while a latecomer, delayed on the Turnpike, hurried to park his car, someone would inevitably ask, "What time does the five o'clock boat leave, Archie?"

Of course, Archie's warmth wasn't reserved for islanders; he had a life off-island which islanders tended to overlook. Maine writer Ken Textor, in an article for *Offshore* (May 1994), quoted one waterfront familiar: "Archie's in love with everything and everyone he's ever come in contact with." Half the trip to Bustins was taken up with long, sweeping waves starting from the shoulder—unmistakable Archie-waves—to lobstermen hauling traps along the route and to a variety of boaters passing by.

Archie lost the *Victory* in 1948; the dramatic story was retold by Textor in an October 2001 *Down East* magazine article. Archie was sitting out a hurricane aboard his boat anchored between Little Bustins and Bustins. He saw another boat dragging anchor, being driven toward the rocks near Pidge's Cove, and he went to its aid. As he tried to take the other boat in tow, a huge wave raised the *Victory* and dropped her right atop some abandoned and hidden underwater pilings that pierced her hull, impaling her

Courtesy of Ben Carr

Archie Ross around 1970.

on the spot. The boat was lost, but islanders flocked to help dismantle the engine that was then taken ashore and its parts dried in an island oven. It would have six more years of life.

Over succeeding months it seemed that islanders and local residents couldn't do enough to help replace Archie's boat. Cash donations poured in, and bake sales and potluck suppers were held to benefit Archie. He added $900 to the cause. In the end $4,000 was raised—enough to build a new boat that Archie would run until he retired in 1996. She was christened to the sound of music played on combs and kazoos by the island teenagers who, wave after wave of them, loved Archie. When launched, her sternboard read *Judas Priest*, but enough dissatisfaction arose to cause her name to be changed to the *Marie L.* after his mother. She was—still is—a beautiful boat. She sat low to the water with a long lean stem and her aquamarine and white paint always looked fresh. Over the years she went through six engines, and she was the first boat in South Freeport to switch to diesel in the early 1950s.

The switch to diesel notwithstanding, Archie, like Ralph Brewer, relied on basic tools and was slow to adopt more modern equipment. Not infrequently fog settled over the bay, making sight navigation impossible. Archie relied on knowledge gained over years of experience—how the tides ran here and there, what the water looked like at a certain point. He combined this knowledge with skillful use of time, compass, and speed. After clearing Pound of Tea he would check his watch, set his compass, and adjust the engine speed until it sounded right. Fifteen or whatever minutes later, the steamer dock on Bustins would loom out of the fog and Archie would ease the *Marie L.* around the edge of the island, and through the moorings to the dock. Passengers never worried, never stopped animated conversations; they knew they were in safe hands.

Over time, more sophisticated navigational instruments appeared and were mandated by the Coast Guard. In 1987, Archie installed radar to pass the annual inspection and eventually used it. He excused the change by noting that his eyes were no longer quite so good, and "There's lots more boats now than there used to be."

Archie's *Marie L.* carried more than passengers and their luggage. All kinds of building material came over on her—lumber and sheets of plywood stacked on the roof, cinder blocks and bags of cement piled toward the stern. Island helpers—Claire Stager, Sue Spalding, Pat Bonney, and Kathie Stager amongst many others—were always on hand to unload and lug. Archie also carried the island mail. When he retired in 1996, he was honored as the nation's longest-running contract carrier and was awarded his own cancellation, a representation of the *Marie L.*, on all envelopes handled by the post office. Archie hauled bottles of propane, generators, and lawn mowers. He carried island trash bound for the Freeport dump or later to the landfill and recycling center. In short, virtually everything that went to or left the island went on Archie's boat.

Archie ran his boat from an upturned Hoods milk box that enabled him to see out his forward windows. At Archie's retirement party, Robbie Boone pointed out the one single design flaw in the *Marie L.*—the deck was set too low.

Because he was both self-sufficient and willing, islanders took Archie too much for granted. We marveled at how he could bring across a load of full propane tanks alone—before the Coast Guard mandated a mate—and hoist them onto the steamer dock. We marveled at the loads of construction materials he ferried across and unloaded. We marveled—and we accepted. Year after year as our children grew and we grew heavier and less agile, Archie seemed ageless. Except for weddings and funerals—and in winter—he was always barefoot.

"I just feel as though I've got to have my shoes off. I just don't feel comfortable otherwise," he said.

His beard never changed, the wrinkles around his eyes from peering into the fog or into the sun never changed. He never lost his bounce.

F. Benjamin Carr

Archie was never ambitious regarding money. He said that he wasn't looking to get rich, he just wanted to support his family. (He had married Jean McElwee in 1953 at a candlelight service in the Community House with 500 guests in attendance; they had three children.) We islanders saw to it that he didn't get rich. For years his contract provided him a guaranteed income. For instance, his contract, signed by Dana Norris for the 1951 season when the *Marie L.* was still brand-new, required of Archie "safe and adequate boat service." In return he was guaranteed $20 a day during the high season. Fares, freight, the mail contract, and any other revenues were to be applied to this figure. No retirement fund existed, no health plan was offered. Archie never complained. Over time improvements were made. The guaranteed-income approach changed to a negotiated subsidy. Archie received the subsidy as well as all the income from the boat. Of course he was responsible for the boat's maintenance, fuel, insurance and other expenses. By 1967, his subsidy was $3,375 for a ninety-day season. The subsidy would continue to rise, as would fares.

A major gain for Archie, a medical plan, came after he suffered a seizure on the boat. He fell and ended up in the hospital. Everyone visited him, but Archie worried about his bills and his worrying hindered his recovery. Winnie Tozier told Archie that money had been raised to pay the bills—and she then set about raising the money. In short order she raised $6,000. Jerry Baker filled in as ferry captain and Archie watched from an upstairs window at the Toziers', buoyed by visits from islanders ("No visitors," the physician had said), good food and lots of rest. He always remembered feeling privileged as he ate swordfish upstairs while the family downstairs supped on hot dogs. With the excess from the funds raised, a health plan was initiated for Archie.

By the 1990s, the Coast Guard required a deckhand. A significant rise in the subsidy occurred when Claire MacDonald, barely approaching middle age, took on the job. After a few years she became Claire Ross, Archie's second wife, and provided him with love and needed structure to his life and diet. She cared for him faithfully until his death. She earned her captain's license and could provide relief for Archie as needed on the *Marie L.* Of course, with all the upgrades to meet Coast Guard regulations, fares were raised, but so was the ferry contract. The contract reached $10,000 in 1992.

Archie, in his early seventies, announced his end-of-season retirement in a letter read at the April 21, 1996, meeting of the Board of Overseers. At the board's next meeting, on May 2, Archie's subsidy was raised from $17,500 to $24,000, plus $5,000 for his retirement fund. While this was a far cry from the figures at which Archie began his fifty years as the Bustins ferryman, it should be noted that when it came time to seek a replacement for Archie, not a single candidate found even the highest subsidy Archie received minimally acceptable.

As Bustins children grew up, married, and had their own children, they carried with them a variety of stories highlighting Archie's kindness and helpfulness. Countless people tell of asking Archie, on the way back to South Freeport, whether he could cash a check for them. "Here's my wallet; take what you need," he would say, passing over his canvas wallet while keeping his eyes focused on the sea ahead. Robbie Boone remembers a summer when he was working on the island truck that met all ferries to haul luggage and passengers. Robbie had made plans to use the family Boston Whaler to leave after the 11:00 a.m. ferry, meet an island girl ashore for a quick lunch and movie, and then be back to meet the 6:00 p.m. ferry. Bud Nickerson would cover for him on the truck. Unfortunately the Whaler wouldn't start. Archie saw Robbie's difficulties, knew of his plans, and said he could squeeze in a special trip to South Freeport before his normal 1:00 p.m. trip from the island. Robbie accepted with alacrity, but worried about the cost of a special trip, an unanticipated expense. As Robbie tells it, "I insisted on paying for the special trip over his [Archie's] objections. He kept protesting as I wrote the check. I included the fare for the 5:00 p.m. trip on which we would be returning. When I handed it to him, he said he wouldn't cash it. I am still waiting for it to clear."

Others tell of Archie's quiet helpfulness. Sue Spalding remembers being eight and telling her grandmother Moore that she knew how to swim—which she didn't—and that she was going to swim from the Public Dock to the closest crib. In she jumped and immediately began floundering. Her brother jumped in after her, and Sue pushed him under. At which point Archie—who couldn't swim a stroke either—grabbed a nearby skiff and yanked her out. She was embarrassed and cried and cried. But Archie was her hero. Archie's wife, Claire, tells of a Chebeague islander whose father had died a few years earlier and who came up to her at Archie's funeral. "We'd never have been able to buy our house if Archie hadn't lent us money," he told her.

Islanders in their seventies remember vividly the moonlight cruises aboard Archie's boat. Middle-aged islanders remember hanging around the Public Dock as youngsters when the boat was due, hoping to tie a line around a cleat or fend off the *Marie L.* as she slid in. Youngsters remember the ice cream trips to Mere Point and being allowed—when Coast Guard regulations were less stringent—to ride on the boat's roof with their legs hanging down over the windshield, blocking Archie's view.

Of course, lots of apocryphal tales swirl in Archie's wake. Over the years a number of islanders chose to have their ashes spread in the bay. Archie, the minister, the mourners, and the ashes would make the trip. Usually Archie, heeding family wishes, chose the spot. But one grieving widower was very particular and was right at Archie's elbow as, on a choppy and breezy afternoon, he took the *Marie L.* out. The man wanted the boat in a particular spot and

Courtesy of Bustins Island Historical Society

Loading the Marie L. at South Freeport. The Marie L. captained by Archie Ross served as the island's ferry from 1950 to 1996.

direction. Archie tried to suggest an alternative, but the man was adamant. The boat was pointed downwind, appropriate words were spoken, and the ashes tipped over the aft side. The breeze picked them up and blanketed the boat—and mourners—with them. Archie said he was days washing off those ashes.

Bud Nickerson, bearded and bigger than life, always told everyone that the diminutive Archie was his son. Archie got the last laugh, according to Winnie Tozier, when her son David flew into the airport and Archie, Olive Nickerson, Winnie and Bud went to meet him. David offered them a ride in his plane. Bud turned green, but Archie loved it and never let Bud forget.

Claire tells of one night when one of her coworkers was visiting them on the mainland and she served a tuna casserole that tasted downright terrible to Archie. He got up from the table and said he was going down to the Harraseeket Lunch to eat. While he was finding the car keys, the coworker slid out the door, casserole in hand, and beat Archie down to the dockside restaurant where, just after his arrival, Archie found a second serving of that same casserole under his nose.

Islanders tell and retell the stories about one frugal islander during Archie's early days. This islander was notorious for wearing as many coats as possible so they wouldn't be classified as luggage, and for tying together any number of odd-sized boxes so they would only count as a single item when it came time to pay. One time he asked whether Archie would tow his skiff across to Bustins. Archie good-naturedly agreed. At the very last moment, just as the boat cast off from the South Freeport dock, the man hopped into the skiff and made the trip perched there. When they reached Bustins, he immediately cornered Archie, informing him that he couldn't be charged full fare because he wasn't aboard. Catering to the man's frugality, Archie promised him a private discount. On every trip the man kept his distance from the other islanders so that his secret would be safe. On every trip Archie whispered into his ear and the man paid, never realizing that he was paying the same rate as every other adult islander on the boat.

The end of the season was always a problem because it included so many good-byes. As Archie is quoted by David Silberbrand in *Marvelous Mainers*, "Fall is the prettiest time of year, but it's the saddest time for me. The houses are closed up; the people are gone. It's like closing a book."

Archie died just short of his seventy-eighth birthday in February of 2002 and was buried on Chebeague on May 22, when a long string of raw, gray days finally gave way to sun and warmth. Brave spring flowers bloomed here and there, including wild blueberries and creeping phlox, or "cemetery pinks." The burial site, close to a tall pine, was carpeted with long brown needles and, protected beneath the outermost tip of its lowest bough, sat Archie's coffin, wooden with rope handles. Quietly, by twos and threes, some aided by walkers, here and there among them a *Marie L.* cap or shirt, Chebeague islanders, with Bustins folk interspersed, gathered to honor their own. There was quiet chatting and many hugs for friends not seen over a long winter and for returners, some of whom had crossed from Cousins Island aboard a resplendent *Marie L.* After the graveside service, flowers were placed on the coffin before everyone crossed the road to the island church for a bountiful luncheon spread prepared by island ladies.

For fifty years, Archie did what he did for its own sake, not for what it would gain him. He asked of life only that he might ply the waters of Casco Bay barefoot and without falling overboard. In the process he served generations of islanders year in and year out. He was the friend of all, a special Maine man whose honesty marched ever before him, a man whose character made him a giant at every turn, a man woven into the warp and woof of each Bustins family.

Chapter Five

The Fifties

IN THE GLORY days of the 1950s, Archie Ross and his *Marie L.* were both young. Ralph and Lilly Brewer were island superintendents and caretakers. A handful of vehicles had the island roads to themselves. Ralph had his old Chevy pickup. Art Henderson drove a Model T Ford, originally brought to the island across the ice in the 1920s by John Jaynes. It had a dump bed and was used to haul gravel for roads. As the century ended it was still rolled out for weddings and parades by owner George Richardson. John had also used a Model A Ford, but it was gone by the 1950s. The Smokers, who owned and operated the store and restaurant for many years, had a truck or two that young John used to deliver groceries. In the 1950s the Hatches and Norrises brought a Jeep to the island. They leased a ship-to-shore radio and provided phone service to the mainland. Later in the decade, David Norris used a black sedan to provide an island taxi service. The largest island vehicle was a 1929 fire truck donated by Freeport after Art Henderson's cottage burned in 1950. The truck was eventually returned to Freeport where, restored, it shone at Firemen's Musters. The island fire department also had a few hand-drawn chemical tanks, antiquities with big wheels.

Until 1958 the Eugene Smoker family ran the store and lived in Rocky Nook across the street. The store occupied what is today the adult library. Smoker spent winters as chef and steward on yachts in Florida and returned north to Bustins in late spring. He provided delicious oatmeal bread, tasty baked beans, and many other delicacies, including ice cream. Mrs. Smoker and daughter Pat worked there, too. Son John was responsible for unloading freight from the ferries, meeting the mail boat *Joan* from Portland, and delivering groceries and milk to island cottages. Grampy Smoker sat for hours on the store porch rolling odd lengths of string onto an ever-larger ball and happily opining, "Ain't it the truth," to any and every comment made within his hearing.

Until 1951, the Smokers' restaurant, Ships Inn, now home to the Bustins Island Historical Society, served three meals every day of the week—except for Sunday supper. Eugene hired his friend Walter Mason as cook and provided him living quarters over the store. Walter was famous for his black-bottom pies. The dishwasher—Al "Scalding" Spalding in the restaurant's final years—lived below where the Emergency Room now is. His

Collection of Freeport Historical Society
The Ships Inn restaurant and the post office in the mid-1900s.

roommate was John Smoker. They were awakened each morning by the sound of Eugene's feet thumping on the dining room floor above. Al earned $12 a week, at the end, plus room and board. But the best pay, as Al notes, was being able to spend the summer on Bustins.

The restaurant relied on many island regulars, including Dr. and Mrs. Eugster, Mr. and Mrs. Hunziker, Mrs. Walton, Miss Potts, and Miss Ethel Swann, along with her nephew Billy and niece Ruthie. The kitchen staff and waitresses especially could barely contain themselves when the salad course was peanut butter-stuffed prunes, on lettuce, of course. The workers craned over one another's shoulders to peek through the kitchen doors and were in stitches watching diners trying to appear nonchalant and unflustered as their tongues worked to scrape out the prune and peanut butter stuck to the roofs of their mouths. Archie Ross also took his meals at the restaurant. Because of his schedule, he often ate alone—and he didn't always like what Walter served. When opportunity offered, he would surreptitiously slip his plate to Al who would in turn edge over to the garbage pail in the kitchen and clean it off. Al and Archie had an active and ongoing collaboration.

Utilities were always a critical issue for islanders. Most cottages in the 1950s still had outhouses. Drinking water was drawn by hand pumps from private wells or from wells located by the store, at George Richardson's, at Indian Springs near the Wade cottage, at the golf course, and at Ewing's ice pond. Rainwater was collected into barrels for dish washing and bathing; most gray water simply drained into the ground beneath the cottages or was piped into the bay. Lots of folks took bars of soap when they went swimming. No deep wells had been drilled. A few islanders were experimenting with newly installed propane gas lamps for light and were slowly changing from iceboxes to propane fridges and from kerosene to propane stoves. Gasoline and kerosene came from Portland on the small tanker *Gulf of Maine*. The gasoline was piped from the Public Dock to the pump that still stands, ancient and rusty now, by the store. Each winter until 1953 Ralph Brewer cut ice in the two small ponds by the Ewing and Leland icehouses and stored it, well-sawdusted, for summer use. But each year Ralph delivered less and less ice, less and less kerosene, and ever-increasing numbers of the 100-pound propane tanks. Large, noisy generators were being used by a small number of families, including the Taiseys, Brainards, Bakers, and Blaisdells, and the Smokers for their store. Some remember the deafening noise of a neighbor's inadequately muffled generator running night after night below their bedroom windows.

Garbage was a recurrent problem. Its disposal provided a summer job for a teenager hired by the Board of Overseers. By long-standing practice it was collected and rowed out to the vicinity of Garbage Ledge—the name still used by many oldsters for what the charts call Bustins or Bibbers Ledge—where it was dumped into the sea or onto the rocks for the seabirds to scavenge. Paper bags might be broken open en route to provide easier access for seagulls whose scavenging skills assured that, in a day when packaging was minimal, little garbage would float ashore. Wastewater flowed through pipes from many cottages to the shore to mix with the waters of Casco Bay. For the cleanliness of the beaches, it was important that the pipes be long enough to reach beyond the low-water mark.

Following the disruptions of World War II, Annual Meetings resumed in the Community House. A newly framed Honor Roll hung in a corner, recognizing those of the Bustins community—including my father—who served their country. The basic village corporation structure of island government was little different from the one used today. Elected members of the Board of Overseers donated their time and expertise for terms of three years. Only the clerk was required by law to be a Maine resident.

F. Benjamin Carr

Neither a planning board nor a zoning board of appeals existed. Nor were board meetings held monthly as they are today. Nor did islanders receive the extensive agendas and minutes circulated today by e-mail. Island business had little to do with Freeport—much less with the state. Each year designated overseers attended the Freeport budget meetings to request a load of gravel for the roads or lumber and chain for repairs to a dock. That was about it. A couple meetings per year sufficed to handle island business and exhaust the annual budget that in those years was less than $5,000.

Most families relied on the ferry to get them on and off the island. Bud Nickerson had a Herreshoff H-28 sailboat, the *Moana*. The Ingham Baker family bought *Whimmy* with its beautifully varnished teak hull in 1954. The classic and fast old catboat *Allegro* arrived on the island in 1960 and lay to its mooring off the Kitchin cottage. Hardly a boat in the bay could beat her downwind, according to owner Charlie Kitchin. Stuart MacDonald had his first *Panacea*. Some families had Pow-Wows—16-foot centerboard sloops with lapstrake hulls that were used for racing or family picnics. Many old-time islanders remember the Pow-Wows fondly as the boats on which they learned to sail. Lew Ward had an old Hampton boat that he occasionally filled with youngsters for a berrying trip to Goose Island. The ubiquitous outboards of today were decidedly not in fashion: They were expensive, somewhat unreliable, and required little skill to operate when compared to the nautical skills needed in a sailboat.

Bustins was green, though the crown of the island was not as high as it would become when enthusiasm for saving trees made tree harvesting and shorefront trimming an island issue. Heavily wooded with tinderbox cottages crowded together along the shore, Bustins was most fortunate that cottage fires never spread to adjacent cottages or the island itself. Art Henderson's cottage burned in 1950, the MacMillan cottage, Wychmere, burned in 1954, and the Zarbock cottage burned in 1959. But when

The Public Dock, mid-1900s.

Collection of Freeport Historical Society

islanders looked across to Lower Goose, what might happen was clear to all. Except for a portion surrounding a cottage at the eastern end, saved by the efforts of volunteers, the island's vegetation had been leveled by a fire that burned for days in 1941. Maine itself suffered wildfires statewide in the fall of 1947 at the end of an extremely dry summer. Thousands of acres in the Waterboro area were devastated; the smell of smoke was carried over Bustins by southwest winds, and sunsets were deep red from smoke in the air. The fire that received the most publicity was, of course, the one that burned across Acadia National Park on Mount Desert Island and forced the evacuation of Bar Harbor.

Other natural disasters also threatened. Hurricane Carol struck in August 1954. After the storm Mrs. Walton, who owned

F. Benjamin Carr

Point of View by the steamer dock, typed a letter to her daughter Peg in which she described Hurricane Carol as seen from her cottage. The following abridged copy of that letter was prepared by Nickie Kitchin for inclusion in the Bustins Island Historical Society's winter 1997 newsletter:

"Dear Peg: Perhaps you will say it is a judgment on me for my years of morbid interest in hurricanes, but at last I've been through one and I have no desire to experience another! Yesterday morning the radio reported that 'Carol' had changed course, built up force and was headed toward N.Y., Cape Cod and Maine. When I got up at 8 yesterday it was calm and water serene, but by 10 o'clock the wind had risen to quite a blow from the Southeast. Kenny Roberts came down to see how my boat was riding and we decided that it couldn't be in a better place than just out here in front, on the mooring. The wind was rising fast, the radio was giving fifteen minute reports on the storm, and things began to look very serious. Archie came back from So.F. at 10:30 and moored on the buoy at Little Bustins. Then the procession began—first Stew's new Islander, then Jaynes', Ward's, skiffs, sailboats, Barnard's 'Peg III,' and at last Dick Taisey's lovely cruiser. Archie tried to get Stew's as it passed near him and then Dick's, but with no luck. Jean was on the boat with him and they both had on orange life jackets as neither could swim. People were down here all day watching Archie and praying, you may be sure. Trees were down all over the place and boys with power saws and axes were trying to keep the roads clear. Still my boat was riding it out, the only one left except Archie's. At 4:45 it was all right, at 4:55 it had started north toward those ledges opposite Burnham cove. After about 200 yards it stopped. I could see it was still on the mooring, was dragging that 250 block, anchored with heavy chain that I had insisted Ralph put it on. At 4:30, with wind in the south, it blew harder and harder. I really thought the roof might

A Maine Summer Island: The Story of Bustins

Collection of Freeport Historical Society
The Public Dock, probably in the 1950s.

go, so I went upstairs and packed all my important papers, jewels and money in a suitcase, brought it down and put it in the dining room with my rubber boots, slicker and sou'wester. If the roof went, I could pick up my luggage and walk out!

"At 6:30 it seemed as if the wind was letting up a bit. There were streaks of perfectly beautiful blue sky to the south, and still how it blew! Just about 7:30 Archie started off and went on to So. Freeport where he and Jean spent the night.

"The tide was high at 1:30 but it stayed up for 2 hours, over the boards of the dock and spray breaking over the road. The new runway, lower half, of Public Float went out, and the float, new this year, hung by one chain, banging on the rocks all night. The outer crib of Barnard's went and the new, half finished runway of the new Brainard Landing disappeared completely. Trees are down everywhere, flower and vegetable gardens, as well as shrubs, are whipped, burned, and laid flat. The lilacs back of the house look as if a flame thrower had been played on them. The windows, both upstairs and down, were so coated with salt you would have thought they had been whitewashed. I put the hose on the lower one and now I can see the water. The shingles on east and south side stood up like a hen's feathers in a blow, and some of them are on the ground this A.M. but not as many as at other houses. No mail or provisions from Portland for the first time in well over 25 years. Today mail came but no milk!

"As you may imagine my house was mecca for the Island yesterday, and they were here, on porch and in the house by droves. Well, we survived and I have seen a hurricane, but no more, thank you." In ink at the bottom of the letter is scrawled "wind 86 mph with gusts up to 100."

On Bustins in 1950 church services were held each Sunday in the Community House. A few hymns were sung, prayers were offered, and an islander, guest or regular, ordained or not, delivered a brief message. As time passed and people found their Sunday afternoons complicated by boat outings, sailboat races, or preparations for leaving the island, the Sunday-afternoon services languished. They finally evolved into a well-publicized annual service down by the Public Dock on an August Sunday morning. Attendance was strong and lots of congregational participation invited. For many years Paul Eckel, with support from Sue Spalding and others, was the popular leader of these annual services, that were followed by fruit juice and fresh doughnut holes from Dunkin' Donuts, provided by Jan Eckel.

Island social life was vibrant and casual. Later the Cottagers Association of Bustins Island, once the Bustins Island Cottagers Association, and the island's governing group before the island became a village corporation in 1913, would sponsor events for both island youth and adults. The members sponsored the annual Field Day with its competitions, square dances, pancake breakfasts, and a plethora of activities. But that would be later. Later, too, would be the creation of the Bustins Island Historical Society, which would present summer exhibits and would invite speakers for its annual meetings. But in the years around 1950 the Rev. Scotty Campbell organized the annual Fourth of July ham and bean supper at the Community House. This event brought the whole island community together and symbolized, in a way, the unity of islanders. On infrequent occasions an island wedding would also bring islanders together. In one such memorable ceremony in 1948, Miriam Wade was married to Charles Butts on the lawn of the Wade cottage. Among attendees were Wally and Joyce Baker, honeymooning on Bustins following their own marriage a week earlier ashore.

Mail was also an occasion for socializing. Each day islanders of all ages met and chatted along the road or while they waited outside the store for the mail. Golfers met at the course for an early-morning round. The serious cribbage players proudly exhibited business cards proclaiming them members of the "15-2" club. Entertaining neighbors and friends for dinner was an integral part of summer, as were late-afternoon gatherings on cottage porches where the rockers creaked back and forth and ice clinked in glasses as island issues were animatedly discussed. The beauty of this "neighboring" was that no invitation was needed. If a porch sported a gathering of people, or even if it was nearly empty, any passerby was welcome to join. This casualness remains a hallmark of the Bustins family.

The young people of the island were seldom at a loss for entertainment. Each morning Paul Wade, or later others, perhaps Langdon Hatch, Phil Campbell, or Dave Harris, followed by a gaggle of younger people, made the rounds to fill the Coleman-lamp streetlights with white gas; at dusk they returned to light them. Some lights stayed lit all night while the flame in others died within the hour. Grass needed cutting. At the Ships Inn, Al Spalding anchored the dishwashing staff with Nat

F. Benjamin Carr

Malloy, Alice Baker, Pat Smoker, Frisky Teal, and Jan LaFleur serving stints as waitresses. Teenagers messed around in small boats, swam from the Public Dock or in Pidge's Cove, hauled crab traps from the various island docks, and caught mackerel to be peddled door-to-door in a galvanized pail. A ready market existed for freshly dug clams. Some teens carried water for older neighbors or puttied windows. Betty Jennison Brady went "tipping"—collecting tips from the branches of balsam firs—for needles to fill the fragrant pillows she made to sell, each bearing the message GREETINGS FROM BUSTINS ISLAND, MAINE.

Faith Dennett and her friend Meg Hutchins ran a small business, Baking-to-Go. Lois Dennett recalls "noisy" games of 52 Scatter with the Bakers, Wades, Perrys, Kitchins, Leonards, and Knights. The young people played tennis and circled the island along the rocks at low tide. Girls wore pedal pushers or broomstick skirts and peasant blouses. Boys wore dungarees and T-shirts.

The Teen-Agers of Bustins Island formed, elected officers and chose A. B. LaFleur to be advisor to the group. The teenagers raised money for games and equipment by selling candy and staging scavenger hunts. Mickey LaFleur and Alice Baker were charged with planning a play and Paul Wade with organizing a softball team to play Dick Braddock's "Old Men." A rota was established to keep the messy game closet clean. Tuesday and Thursday nights were game nights at the Community House— mostly Ping-Pong and chatting. Some played musical instruments; some sang. Saturday night was dance night. Everyone brought records with them from home and, with the power from the generator cranked up next door in the old schoolhouse, they played the records on a Victrola. A few chaperones were present; favorites were young couples like Tish and Glen Guernsey and Dick and Gloria Braddock, barely out of their teens themselves, who joined in as the young folks fox-trotted, waltzed, and occasionally jitterbugged. The hits of the time included "I

Can Dream, Can't I?" featuring the Andrews Sisters, Doris Day singing "Bewitched," and Sammy Kaye doing "Harbor Lights." Other hits were "Tennessee Waltz" by Patti Page, "Mona Lisa" by Nat King Cole, "Wheel of Fortune" by Kay Starr, "Music, Music, Music" by Teresa Brewer, "Because of You" by Tony Bennett, and "Any Time" by Eddie Fisher.

Outside of structured events, the teenagers did a lot of singing, both down by the store porch and around the island. Music nights were frequent at the Baker-Wade cottage. Jamie Hancock, a few years older and the idol of island young people, took part. So did Frisky Teal on the glockenspiel and ukulele popularized by Arthur Godfrey. Al Spalding strummed the banjo, and Alice Baker her guitar. Cowboy songs—"Red River Valley" and others—were popular. "Georgia on My Mind" always targeted Georgia Gates. Later, as they circled the island, "Show Me the Way to Go Home" might be followed by "We Were Sailing Along on Casco Bay," to the delight of all except those trying to get to sleep.

Teenagers looked forward to the moonlight cruises with Archie on the *Marie L.* They always hoped that a dense fog would swoop in and they would be marooned overnight in some distant cove—as on occasion they were. Once in a while someone would organize an overnight camping trip to a neighboring island. Everyone, adults and young alike, looked forward to the Bustins Bust, an annual event in which outlandish costumes, corny acts, and zany music with words adapted to the island scene convulsed everyone in attendance, including the performers themselves. The boys had a ball team; periodically the Freeport team would come to play the islanders.

Age consciousness was a constant factor governing social activities. While everyone knew everyone, of course, young people seldom strayed from their own age group. They would socialize neither with a younger sister's group nor an older brother's group. So the island was tiered with small age-specific cliques. Summer romances, occasional skinny-dipping, and a bottle of hard-to-come-by beer were all part of a Bustins summer for youngsters. A visit to Freeport as part of a day ashore was less daunting than it might be today, and teenagers looked forward to occasional trips to the Nordica movie theater or the bowling alley. The town had not yet become a shopping mecca crowded with chain outlet stores, restaurants, sidewalk vendors, and a camouflaged McDonalds'. In the 1950s, the train still came through the middle of town on its way eastward.

L.L. Bean, then as now, played a central role in Freeport's economy. But, though already at its present location, it was a different L.L. Bean. To reach it, a shopper walked through the double doors to the left of the tile-fronted post office, climbed the stairs to the second floor, and passed through another set of doors into the boot-work area. Beyond lay more stairs leading to the office and stitching area—and the salesroom to which celebrities as varied as Eleanor Roosevelt and Ted Williams found their way.

In South Freeport, the houses along Main Street, Harraseeket Road, and Park Street were still owned by longtime Freeporters who had been ship captains, bootleggers, or fishermen. Along with their Bustins cottages, John Jaynes and Al Guppy both owned houses on its shaded streets. The small cottages on Park Street—there were six of them—had been company houses for shipyard workers. Majestic elms overarched Main Street, although they would soon die of Dutch elm disease. Without them the street seemed naked and forlorn. The post office, located at the top of the hill opposite the end of Harraseeket Road, would soon move up around the corner to the Village Store, adjacent to the present post office.

Driving in the other direction, down the hill to the boatyard and water, a long scruffy boatyard building, with many doors and used for winter boat storage, provided summer automobile storage for Bustins people. The rate was $30 for the season. The South Freeport Yacht Basin, run by the Harry Parker family, had no travel lift yet and was much more modest in facilities and services. A second boatyard, run by the Ring family, and the predecessor of today's Strouts Point Wharf Company, didn't open until 1969. It would compete with Harraseeket Marine Services, operated by the Bakers, who took over from the Parkers. The Bakers purchased the Soule Building from Bill Soule and bought the welded ship sculpture that sat atop the building for so many years and is now above the entrance to the main building of Brewer South Freeport Marine. The harbor itself had relatively few pleasure craft on moorings, and none of the large diesel-powered fiberglass fishing boats that today load bait and unload catches of lobster at the docks beside the Town Landing. In the 1950s Archie and Jean Ross ran the Daggers Edge Restaurant on the waterfront. In the 1970s, on filled land rented to them by the Bakers, John Coffin and his family opened the Harraseeket Lunch. This new enterprise quickly drew cars and recreational vehicles full of tourists to enjoy a seafood meal and take photos of a busy Maine harbor and fishing docks.

For those who live there today, the present tends to become all encompassing. Its sweep is worldwide and to keep up with it is a greater challenge than most of us can meet. We are so swept up in the present that we find it difficult to grasp clearly that there has ever been a past when things were different. Some old homes remain along with some old trees, meetinghouses, cemeteries, and quaint street names.

Fifty years ago, tourists and residents alike experienced a Maine vastly different from the Maine they find today, with its interstates, malls, elegant homes, lawn and gardening services, and tourist attractions. For a long time, as the late island centenarian Frank Garfield reminisced to Sue Spalding, the mainland moved forward when the island didn't. Now the island hurries to catch up.

F. Benjamin Carr

Glimpses

Summer

Sunrise before five in line with the island edges between our Lookout bed and Mere Point

Kirklands rolling the tennis courts and putting down the tapes

Wild geraniums blooming on the way to the golf course

Warbler migration filling the trees with flashing colors

Fathers and sons heading for the golf course

Green and white WELCOME flag hanging outside the Ships Inn Museum

Courtesy of Dean L. Lunt

Cove on the west side of Bustins Island.

A Maine Summer Island: The Story of Bustins

Seat reservations scrawled on the paper tablecloths for the Fourth of July ham and bean supper

"Oohs" and "aahs" at our fireworks display with Portland's show a distant backdrop

Strings of baby eiders, fuzz-balls learning to dive and skitter across the surface, under the watchful eyes of clucking mothers

Field Day with spectators cheering on children and grandchildren

Seconds on blueberry pancakes at the Cottagers Association of Bustins Island pancake breakfast

Courtesy of Ben Carr

The 1920 Ford is an annual participant in the Fourth of July parade.

F. Benjamin Carr

Lobster pot buoys on the bay as thick and bright as wildflowers in an alpine meadow

Yellowthroats nesting in the puckerbrush

Morning fog turning yellow before the sun burns it away

The island haloed with boats large and small, power and sail

Ruth Pease at eighty-something mowing her lawn and chatting up passersby

Young people and their visitors, some faces known and others not, on the roads and shore rocks

Al Spalding, with banjo, leading his aging Royal River Philharmonic cronies in concert at the Community House

Grands vying with catbirds and song sparrows for not-quite-ripe raspberries in the front yard

Flashlight tag and Ultimate Frisbee at night on the golf course

Summer love, ever new and ever old

"Do not wash: This vehicle undergoing a scientific dirt test." With clattering propane tanks, the gasman cometh

Mares' tails across the sky foretelling an approaching weather change

Stepping-stone look-alike Larsons, like a many-legged centipede, running barefoot to the Lookout

The huge rhododendron in brilliant bloom beside the Brewer cottage

A Maine Summer Island: The Story of Bustins

Courtesy of Dean L. Lunt

Hot day, cool water.

F. Benjamin Carr

Inchworms dangling at eye level from overhanging branches

Mashing succulent raspberries against the roof of the mouth

Puddled paths, sodden pine needles, and drippy branches after days of rain

Colored voting slips held high during Annual Meeting

Crab traps off the steamer dock

Indian paintbrush standing brave before the onrushing lawn mower

Redolent sweet fern along the path to Indian Springs

Outhaul lines hopelessly snarled and wound together by eelgrass and bladderwort after a storm

Thick o' fog, eerie silence broken only by the sound of droplets falling from every leaf

A gull on the rocks, head extended skyward, bugling laughter at the world

Laura doing her power walks and Jim jogging island laps

Annual fire drill: "Excuse me, but your cottage is on fire. What are you going to do?"

Square dances

Family barbecues in the Boone yard featuring succulent smells, abundant food, and high spirits

Scrabble, cribbage, books to beat cabin fever during rainy spells

A Maine Summer Island: The Story of Bustins

Courtesy of Dean L. Lunt
Private docks on the island's west side looking toward Flying Point.

Youngsters circling the island on the rocks at low tide and exploring each tide pool for treasure

Islanders nattering idly in the sun outside the post office while they wait for Olive to sort the mail

Sunning on the rocks and swimming at the cove

The musical warning from Fred Pease's ancient pickup as he heads dump-ward with brush

The Women's Tennis League in full swing

Elaborate forts built by young warriors to defend against pirates— or alien invaders

A collusion of bicycles outside the Martin cottage

Charlie's voice audible above the sound of his outboard motor as he ferries friends and family to and from the mainland

Youngsters life-jacketed and shrill-voiced aboard the *Marie L*—the "ice cream special" to Paul's Marina on Mere Point

Courtesy of Jan Eckel

Alex learning the game young at the island's tennis courts.

A Maine Summer Island: The Story of Bustins

Bill Grece, dedicated greeter, awaiting the next ferry

George on his red tractor caring for road drainage problems

Barefooted youngsters climbing Turtle Rock for the first time

Afternoon ball games at the golf course, boys performing before seemingly oblivious girls

Island rope swing in use at high tide by daring swimmers of all ages

Water buckets being filled at the island pumps and the island dogs lapping at the overflow

Excited greetings as the ferry disgorges new arrivals—and sad good-byes as the lines are cast off

The Bustins Island post office, 2007.

Courtesy of Dean L. Lunt

F. Benjamin Carr

Courtesy of Ben Carr

The Bustins Island fire truck on an island fire drill day, 2000. Sue Spalding is at the wheel.

Pond lilies behind Leland's icehouse

Gulls, in twos, threes, and fives, silently winging homeward to Green Island Ledges at day's end

Chapter Six

An Electrifying Controversy

FOR YEARS following World War II, Maine remained rural and decentralized by tradition and by choice. Augusta and the long tentacles of state government had not yet become a powerful presence reaching into every corner of the day-to-day business of Maine communities. Islands were seen as burdens rather than as gifts. Lists were circulated of Maine islands seemingly without owners of record. Many could be bought at laughably low prices. In 1947, Marilyn pestered her father to buy Moshiers Island, adjacent to and larger than Bustins, on the market with an asking price of $5,000. (He deflated her dream by asking, as fathers sometimes do, that basic and utterly sensible question: "What would you do with it?")

Despite the seemingly placid surface, however, and despite the seeming ascendancy of the status quo, change was in the air. Change always ignites controversy. Change is always dressed in emotions. One group applauds change they see as overdue. Another group views change as a threat because it alters the accepted, traditional way.

In the late 1960s, Bustins was set to encounter decades of change that would alter our closely held mantra—"Keep Bustins the way it has always been." The challenge was: How to resist change when it seemed important to do so, how to adapt to change when necessary, and, paramount, how to keep our island the way we wanted it in the face of the waves of change that were building. Sometimes we could accept or reject the change. More often, though, we were left to deal with change already enacted elsewhere—through legislation or a changing society ashore whose influence seeped onto the island. In short, sometimes we could choose how we responded, but we couldn't choose whether to respond.

No one anticipated rough waters ahead when, on March 9, 1967, Gov. Kenneth Curtis approved H.P. 111, Legislative Document 138, amending the 1913 Enabling Act that created the Bustins Island Village Corporation. This new document allowed us to raise funds for such needs as a fire department, road repairs, garbage collection, wharves, security, and water, as well as "to produce or procure light for public use and for the use of the inhabitants of the island, and for such purposes to contract with any individual, firm or corporation to furnish such water or light."

All this seemed remote from our perennial hot buttons—the island store, transportation, summer help, and money.

The first wispy mare's tail of what would blow up into a storm came in an August 21, 1967, letter to A. B. LaFleur—Marilyn's dad and a member of the island's Board of Overseers—from G. T. Bell Jr., district manager in Brunswick for Central Maine Power Company. According to longtime islander Winnie Tozier, LaFleur contacted CMP because his wife, Peg, who had a touch of arthritis, wanted an electric blanket.

"In reply to your request for an estimated proposal for electric service to Bustins Island," wrote Bell, "we would like additional time to prepare a proposal. This is a situation beyond the scope of our normal policy."

Nothing further happened during the summer of 1968, but at the Labor Day Weekend 1968 meeting of the overseers, information received from CMP was considered. This is the first formal appearance of any proposal for bringing electricity to Bustins. Recognizing the technical complexities of such a major island undertaking, chairman Ingham Baker requested firmer cost figures that he might include in a letter to all cottage owners. A month later LaFleur wrote Baker that on his last visit with CMP's Bell, he had invited Bob Clark, another member of the Board of Overseers, to accompany him.

After meeting with Bell, and after reflection on the plan, Clark committed himself to the project and, as was his way, immersed himself in its planning and technical details.

"[W]e should move post haste and without further delay to achieve electrification of the island," Clark wrote to the board in an October 16 letter.

A common 100-pound tank of propane gas delivered to an island cottage cost $18 then, and would cool an island refrigerator for three weeks, he calculated. Electricity, he claimed, would cost $2.17 for the same period.

"No wonder gas refrigerators are no longer manufactured!" he wrote.

Baker called a meeting of the overseers for November 3. Baker, Clark, LaFleur, Fred Pease, Roger Leland, and clerk Katherine Needham attended. A plan was adopted that would bring electricity to Bustins. The steps included sending cottagers an outline of the proposal and an authorization sheet. If a simple majority of the sheets were signed and returned, the chairman was authorized "to negotiate with CMP or other contractors as he may see fit for the immediate construction of the system."

All this activity occurred after summer had ended and cottagers had returned to their day-to-day lives. At worst some felt it was a conspiracy, but at the very least it represented a major miscalculation by the overseers, even if undertaken for the best of reasons. The board also erred when it chose to emphasize the financial costs involved while ignoring the emotional impact. On an island where residents were as close as Bustins' claimed to be, board members should have known better and proceeded more cautiously.

Instead, the board planned to move forward with urgency.

"If all goes well," Clark wrote to Needham on November 9, "you will be able to enjoy a shocking experience on Bustins by about June 1."

In fairness, Clark also recognized the inherent dangers of failure, in which case, as he wrote to LaFleur, "we will all be ridden off the island on a rail, tarred and feathered, to join our ancestors in the happy hunting ground!"

Before Thanksgiving the packet entitled "Bustins Electrification: Facts and Proposals" was mailed to cottage owners. Along with what has already been noted, the proposal indicated that $10,000 was the guaranteed maximum cost, and said that the underwater cable carrying 7,200 volts would run from Bustins to Flying Point. Voter eligibility rules were complicated—many would attack them vigorously—and unless more than 50 percent of cottage owners approved by December 21, 1968, the board would take no further action at the time.

LaFleur signed the authorization sheet and asked whether this was the time to sign over his second cottage to his children. The cottage had been bought for the children's use in the first place, and signing it over would "afford us an extra vote for the power," he wrote. Following similar reasoning, other cottagers would sign over woodlots to children in the hope of gaining additional votes. (This strategy would have long-term implications when shoreland zoning was adopted in the mid-1970s.)

The volume of mail to Clark rose dramatically in December. Some islanders raised technical questions. For example:

How safe is year-round service on a summer island?

How big will the cable be?

How will CMP handle the island's many ledges?

Will the cable from Flying Point be trenched or simply laid?

F. Benjamin Carr

Will monthly charges be reduced during the winter?

Many islanders were excited at the prospect of electricity. Jacques Delamarre said that while he and his family had been associated with the island since 1914, they used their cottage infrequently because it lacked facilities.

"Bustins is a delightful place but the Island unfortunately lived for many years in the Dark Ages," he explained. "We feel that with the advent of electricity and telephone, the Island would undergo a long overdue Renaissance."

Correspondence from those opposed dominated, understandable because people are less apt to write in favor of proposals. Opposition took two primary forms: The first focused on how electrification would change Bustins, both physically and in terms of a unique island ambience that many held dear. Not only would electricity present a greater fire hazard than kerosene lamps and gas stoves, according to Windsor Jellis, but "the necessary poles and cable would cut into the beauty and charm of Bustins to such a degree as to spoil it for many who have loved it as long or longer than I."

Jellis said he was incensed by the board's overbearing methods that he deemed a personal insult to his intelligence and integrity.

Georgia Gates, identifying herself as new to the island, asked whether electrification might not lead to increased water use and consequent waste water disposal issues.

Writing on December 2, Bud Nickerson penned an eight-page letter of protest. "As far as I am concerned, it would be the end of Bustins Island as I know it and love it."

Enough damage has already occurred, he noted, at the hands of those who so needed electricity that they had installed generators and others who wanted the island to be no more than an extension of their lives ashore. What is more beautiful, relaxing, and enjoyable, he asked, "than to go to Bustins and sit on your porch or sail your boat or have a clambake or a walk around the island in the evening—and to look at the sunset, the moon, stars, see a storm brewing and wait for it to strike, or wake up to a new fallen snow off season and chop some wood for the fireplace or stove, exhilarating in the fresh air and vigor of the exercise. This is the main thing. Why have people been coming to Bustins for generations and loving it so? Because it is one of the few places left where one can enjoy a simple life this way. Let those who want creature comforts like TV, electric irons, etc. go where it is already abundantly available, and leave at least this one little island to those 'nuts' who want to preserve it the way it is."

Nickerson's timeless plea echoes in many Maine communities.

"Don't think I am condemning you as a newcomer—far from it!" he wrote to Clark. "I like to see new blood coming to Bustins—but I want them to come because they like the 'status quo,' not because they want to change a good thing."

The second target of those opposing electrification was the board's assertion that it could enter into a contract with CMP without voter approval at an Annual Meeting. George Richardson, in a letter dated December 2, said, "After reviewing the By-Laws of the B.I.V.C. [Bustins Island Village Corporation] and recent amendments, it is my opinion that no legal or contractual action can be taken at this time of year. Furthermore, any matter as important as this is to the general character and well-being of the summer residents should be open to discussion at a regular Annual Meeting."

Other islanders registered their opposition in a similar vein. Attached to the letter from Henry Kirkland, former board chairman, was a letter from his lawyer pointing to those articles in the Enabling Act and By-Laws that appeared to raise questions about the board's actions. "Unless I hear from you by December 21, 1968," the lawyer concluded, "I shall assume that you intend to go ahead with this illegal action and shall take Court action to prevent it."

While all this sometimes heated correspondence was occurring, and while Clark was busy defending the board's actions, two other noteworthy actions were initiated, one public and the other less so. On December 7, Chairman Baker wrote a three-page letter to islanders. After noting that votes were running more than 2 to 1 in favor of electrification, he dealt point by point with the issues raised. He also reaffirmed the right of the board to act without a public meeting, and he reiterated the board position that the procedure adopted was "a more stringent test and method of obtaining a true expression than to attempt to consider this complex subject at a Village Meeting."

Behind the scenes, and with the request for an answer "at your earliest convenience," Clark, at Baker's request, wrote on December 5 to Paul Powers of the Freeport law firm of Powers and Bradford. He included copies of the proposal, rehearsed the board's position, acknowledged anxiety about the process, and then got to the point by asking the basic question: "whether the Board (if so voted, on this proposal) may proceed to negotiate a contract with Central Maine Power Co. immediately following Dec. 21 (contract to be made subject to the total receipt of pledged donations), or whether all activity must cease until a formal meeting of the B.I.V.C. had been held."

Powers's response was prompt. He recited the pertinent articles from the Enabling Act and By-Laws and then addressed the core question: "Unless there have been some changes in the charter or by-laws which I have not seen, it is my definite opinion that the Board of Overseers do not have the authority to sign any document which would bind the corporation, in the nature of a contract with the Central Maine Power Company."

The only way this could happen, he continued, would be by a vote in an annual or special meeting to ratify and confirm what the board had done. This was the only way, in fact, that the voters could authorize the overseers in a way that also bound the corporation. Powers concluded by restating his position.

"I would say that if the Board of Overseers want to take the chance of personal liability, and the further chance that the voters in a legal corporation meeting might not vote to ratify and confirm their actions, and make the same the actions of the corporation, then they could go ahead and sign the contract with the power company. If I have not made myself clear, please feel free to write me or call me."

This ended the push for early electrification of the island without a meeting of landowners. Regardless of the legal issues involved, clearly the board did not fully appreciate that people's perceptions needed to be addressed whether or not they seemed uninformed or unfounded.

An elected board, especially on a tight little island, cannot make decisions as the chief executive of a corporation might. Their decisions must be not only economically and technologically sound, but they must also be responsive to the emotions and aesthetic sense of their constituents and be politically acceptable. This last includes timeliness. Obviously many islanders felt the proposal had not been presented in a timely fashion. It provided for no meeting of islanders to share feelings and opinions, no chance for arguments and counterarguments to be heard. It seemed to many that efforts were being made to rush the issue through by polling islanders in isolation during the off-season. These were major miscalculations on the part of a volunteer board whose members, as so many wrote, stood to gain nothing from their support of the proposal and who had at heart only the island's welfare as they saw it.

Clark wrote to CMP's Bell on December 21 that although not all votes were in, it appeared that the necessary 51 percent majority needed to proceed had not been attained. But he felt that a simple majority of voting islanders would approve electrification at a village corporation meeting. He wrote again in the same vein on December 30, citing the need for more study and hoping the CMP planners could prepare a clear contract for consideration by the board and property owners. Then, "perhaps we will be able to conclude this extremely complex matter with a reasonable amount of mutual understanding . . . and hopefully, get the job done as soon as possible."

No tentative time line was mentioned.

Baker wrote to his fellow islanders on Christmas Day, informing them in capital letters that "THE PROPOSAL WAS NOT APPROVED." Some who voted against the proposal did so, he noted, "ONLY because they mistakenly believed that the B.I.V.C. and its Board was involved in an illegal act."

He noted that there were some other legal issues that needed to be addressed, and ended his letter with a wish, "May 1969 bring you happiness and health whether on Bustins or elsewhere." The clear implication is that the push for electrification was dead.

And so 1968, with its tumultuous autumn for islanders, ended.

But not all life had been drained from the proposal. A new board strategy emerged. Roger Leland stepped into the fray on January 2 with a somewhat belated response to Henry Kirkland's lawyer, Frederick Conroy in Lexington, Massachusetts. He disagreed with Conroy's interpretation that the corporation had no power to raise money for the installation of electric light and power. He also went on to foretell a changed strategy by the board to further the electrification plan.

"It has never been the intent of the Board of Overseers," he wrote, "to execute contracts or agreements with Maine Power until after the annual meeting held between July 8th and August 20th, properly called."

He explained that the proposal cottage owners had received was simply informational, and designed to gauge sentiments on the issue. The method was chosen since many, including a number interested in electrification, did not generally attend the Annual Meeting. As for the time deadline, it had been merely for the convenience of some board members who had been available before but not after December 21. If, however, a majority of owners favored power, lots of preliminary work needed to be done before a final proposal was presented at the Annual Meeting. He closed by reaffirming that the board had no wish to go against the will of the people and chided Conroy's client.

"Henry, of all people, should know how much work is involved in just the everyday run of island business without undertaking a project such as this one," he wrote.

New breath was pumped into the project.

Early in the new year, Clark was back at his typewriter. In a letter to LaFleur he reflected weariness at his role as lightning rod for the islanders' views. Your name is "Bustins Mud," he wrote, and opponents "are attempting to organize your AND my removal from the Board. La de da!" However, he predicted that the island would vote for electrification while returning the board to office.

He offered this advice to LaFleur, "DON'T get emotionally involved. AVOID the issue like the plague. BE A GHOST . . . nobody can fight a figment of the imagination . . . although they attempt to raise in the imagination of others an image of their opponent as a terrible demon . . . a la Don Quixote. In short, those who are the most violently negative are perhaps a little bit sick too."

Despite his frustrations, Clark's commitment, emotional and other, continued. Over the ensuing winter months, he corresponded with Powers and numerous others as the board prepared for a renewed effort to secure the island's electrification.

Various islanders were enlisted in the effort. Hunt Burr marshaled reasons for electrification. Bill Barrows submitted a rough draft of a letter to islanders supporting the initiative. The necessary machinery was put in place to move toward a special meeting of the village corporation. A committee of non-board members—Wally Baker, Hunt Burr, and John Mellecker—was established, calling itself the Bustins Electrification Committee.

A big step forward came in an April 23 mailing. A five-page packet included a three-page cover letter, a Plan of Action to Finance Electrification, and a pledge sheet. The informational material referred to the polling of cottage owners the previous fall, in which those favoring electrification had not reached the board's self-imposed level for continuing electrification.

In the final count, thirty-eight owners of forty-two cottages voted for electrification, twenty-eight owners of twenty-nine cottages voted against, and twenty owners of twenty-eight cottages did not vote. Inasmuch as a majority of those voting had thought electricity would make their island time more enjoyable, the electrification committee had been formed to see how power could be made available to those who wished it. Success would require two fundamental accomplishments: raising money by the electrification committee to finance installation of cable, poles and lines; and approval of a number of necessary steps by the village corporation membership at a special meeting on July 19.

In the mailing, islanders were categorized as those wanting power now or later; those not wanting power for their own cottages but not opposed to power being available for those who wanted it; and those who opposed power for themselves and for others. Reasons for electrification followed, a listing culled from letters noted earlier: convenience, reduced fire hazard, lower operating expense, improved public lighting for recreation and safety, better refrigeration at the store. Each was explained before the mailing concluded that "Electricity for the island is inevitable—sooner or later." Delaying would only increase costs. The reasons for not introducing electricity were also listed without explanation.

The Plan of Action to Finance Electrification was straightforward. The electrification committee sought a $200 pledge from each cottage owner by May 10. If pledges were sufficient to cover anticipated installation costs, the committee would request that the village corporation call a special meeting on July 19. If the voters approved electrification at the special meeting, pledges would be due and the committee would give the corporation the money needed for installation, including the underwater cable.

Thirty-seven cottage owners responded positively to the mailing, pledging the $200. This encouraged Baker and Clark, along with Needham, to meet with Paul Powers in Freeport on May 19 to discuss the form and wording of the call for a special meeting that would be forthcoming and the articles for the meeting—although the board had not yet received a formal request for the meeting. (This request came May 29.) The Bustins Electrification Committee (BEC) was satisfied enough with the results obtained to request that the Board of Overseers call a special meeting of the corporation on July 19 to vote on electrification and on whatever resolutions were needed to achieve it.

Even before the request for a special meeting had been made or the call issued, the paper war resumed. Charlie and Nickie Kitchin began it with a six-page letter to Bustins islanders dated May 21. They had thought the issue dead when the BIVC failed the previous autumn to muster a simple majority favoring electrification. Their letter stressed that islanders were a race apart with a most estimable New England trait: "GUMPTION." They extolled the island's beauty and tranquility and emphasized the need to protect it for posterity. "[H]ow do you think your sons, grandsons, or nephews will feel," they asked, "coming home from the jungles of Vietnam to find Bustins a Casco Bay Long Island?" They foresaw bitterness continuing over the issue and pled for islanders "to keep our island the way it is."

In his letter, Stuart MacDonald referred to a number of older residents who opposed electrification but who voted for it or abstained so as not to seem against progress. "If progress is the hippie, the sit-in, SDS, LSD, the campus takeover, the southeast expressway—the longer we resist progress on Bustins, the better off we will be . . . If we want all the creature comforts of home, why not stay home or, as an alternative, try Cape Cod?"

Meanwhile, Baker and Needham met with Powers on June 17 to discuss who would be eligible to vote at the special meeting. Powers's opinion was that Section 9 of the Enabling Act, repeated in Article VI of the by-laws, defined legal voters first as those within the limits of the corporation, Bustins Island, who would, if they lived in Freeport, qualify to be legal voters in Freeport—meaning those listed as legal voters in the town office and residing on Bustins; and second, as every person of legal age (twenty-one years of age for males, and under twenty-one if a married female) owning a part or the whole of one or more lots on Bustins. A person with a legal deed, signed, sealed, witnessed and acknowledged before a justice of the peace or notary public, was an owner even if the deed was not yet recorded in the Registry of Deeds.

The final board meeting convened at Baker's Bustins Island cottage on June 29. Baker, Clark, Leland, and Needham were present, while Pease and LaFleur were absent. The upcoming special meeting was discussed. Powers would attend, along with representatives of CMP and New England Telephone. A list of eligible voters, based on an April 1 listing of Freeport voters, would be posted. A form would be available to be signed by anyone not listed who felt entitled to vote. A credentials committee would consist of the chairman, the clerk, and one other member appointed by the chairman at the meeting. Non-voters would be seated together, and Freeport authorities would be asked to provide a police officer.

The special meeting of the Bustins Island Village Corporation began at noon on July 19. Dana Norris, reportedly opposed to electrification, was chosen moderator rather than Bob Dennett, reportedly in favor of electrification. A motion was made and seconded on the second article to the effect that the corporation accept a gift of $10,000 from the electrification committee to purchase and install the underwater cable and to pay the excess costs (beyond those normal for a rural installation) of providing electric service to the island.

In the discussion that followed, the reasons for the BEC were reviewed by Wally Baker, as well as how financing would occur. He summarized reasons for and against electrification, touched on refrigeration, and made some pointed comments. He was deeply concerned about an island split over the issue, concerns justified by the fact that twice, CMP stakes—positioned to help islanders see where poles would be placed—had been maliciously pulled out, and by the suspicion that opponents had split lots or deeded woodlots to friends and other non–cottage owners to create a bloc of votes. Such "bill of sale" transfers could be enrolled following the meeting.

"If, indeed, such lots are voted, it would be deceptive, a travesty of the democratic process which could disguise the true wishes of cottage owners," he said. "Those who use this 'ballot box stuffing' will deserve to lose the friendship of the rest of the island."

Baker concluded that if the vote passed, pledges should be sent to him, and he hoped that those who decided to electrify in the future would also contribute their proportion to the original cost—thus reducing the share for all.

Discussion raged for two hours and forty-five minutes. Zealous teenagers, opposed to electrification, petitioned to preserve the status quo. The authorities—Powers, Bell, and the New England Telephone representative—discussed the emotional questions thrown at them with as much patience, understanding, and calmness as they could muster. Those questions were relatively few, however; most of the discussion was back and forth between islanders.

The Times Record in Brunswick announced the results to the world: "Bustins Island, a mile-long point of land sporting 99 summer cottages and one year-round resident, will go without electricity a few more years. By a vote of 46 to 59, cottage owners at town meeting on the island rejected last Saturday an article designed to speed construction of an electric cable between the island and the mainland."

With the failure of this article, the others became moot.

Some, like Marilyn Larson, were disappointed. "It seemed like it was time to keep up with progress."

Others, like Chairman Baker, thought to continue the campaign.

"While the issue is closed for this season," he wrote in his thank-you note to Bell, "I believe it is still in the minds of many." Baker felt that more specific information about burying lines, including costs, might have made a difference.

"Can you not plan to go into this matter and submit the figures to me?" he asked.

The majority, however, whatever the underlying reason for their particular vote, could take pleasure in *A Plea for the "Status Quo"* circulated by Bud Nickerson on the eve of the special meeting.

"They're talking about 'LECTRIKIN' Bustins,
    the island we've all grown to love,
they're saying how E-lectric power will solve all the problems we have.
They're saying we've just got to have it, it can't be avoided, you know;
and yet I can hear a loud murmur that seems to be saying 'GO SLOW.'
Just think of what you'll be losing by bringing that foreigner in,
and realize that once you have done it, you can't send him home again.
Yes, this is the main thing, I'm thinking, here by the oil lamp's glow,

Just how do we send him a-packing, if we don't like his gaudy show?
Can we say, 'Go home, Lectric power, we've tried you and now must admit
We didn't appreciate our island until we had ruined it?'
NO! We'll have burned all our bridges, we can never make a new start,
For Bustins is not just an island, it's a feeling that grows in the heart.
There are so many vacation places, where modern conveniences hold sway,
So, why not leave this one island for the nuts who like it this way?
Let's chop our wood and haul water, let's read by the gaslight's soft gleam,
let's come down here in chilly December and see the new snow's soft sheen.
Let's not detract with poles and wires, let's not hack up trees and brush,
let's let Bustins be our retreat spot from this high-stepping world's mad rush.
And let's be proud we made this decision, let's tell our children we heard
their plea to keep Bustins Island a place where contentment's the word.

Some continued to hold out hope for electrification before long; some found that strains between themselves and others stretched out into the succeeding generation; some found a ready topic for reminiscence and debate over a drink as they watched approaching dusk on one porch or another. Most were relieved that their summer lives could return to normal.

Resisting change marketed as progress is never simple. I came to believe that the majority of islanders, from Bud Nickerson to the teenagers, were on target with their opposition. In hindsight they seem clairvoyant: all the conveniences that electrification promised are available today—without underwater cables, poles, wires, and bills—through solar panels and storage batteries.

The first wave of change had crashed against the Bustins shore, and its spume had been flung high. The energy powering this wave had emerged from within the island. Other waves that would follow were powered by forces from beyond.

Chapter Seven

Financing a Summer Island

BUSTINS Island became a village corporation by act of the state legislature in 1913. This entitled it to a measure of financial and administrative autonomy. But at the same time Bustins remained part of Freeport to which it pays taxes. Each year the island sought an appropriation of funds to help cover the expenses of running and maintaining the island. Basically, each year the island's Board of Overseers went to the town with its request for funding to pay for road repair or dock repair or other costs. And each year, how much the island requested was a surprise to the town and how much it would receive was a surprise to Bustins. While frustrating, the process worked for a long time. But as the cost of running the island increased dramatically in the later part of the twentieth century—in part because of increasing government regulations—the need for change grew increasingly critical.

During the 1950s, the costs were small and island operations relatively informal.

The handwritten minutes of the island's 1951 Annual Meeting show that G. E. Ramsdell (who owned the present Dennett cottage) was clerk and Judge Burnett was moderator.

Reports were received from the Sanitation Committee (Charlie Kitchin), the Landscape Committee (Arthur Silver), and the Fire Department (Chet Deering). Kitchin reported that all wells had been tested, but some failed. Deering reported that

$632 had been spent for fire equipment. Expenditures also included $186.68 for roads, $5.00 for legal fees, and $991.05 for repairs to the island float and runway. For the year, twenty-nine checks were issued. The total money raised was $4,311.76. Bustins received $2,500 from Freeport, with the additional $1,800 provided by a loan from the Cottagers Association of Bustins Island and monies from the association's Fire Fund. By no stretch of the imagination was island business a major financial undertaking or time commitment.

Throughout the 1950s most of the same committees continued to function. The island contracted to buy the old Freeport fire engine #2—a 1929 Chevrolet. Islanders were exhorted to learn how to use it in case of emergency. The island was being reassessed for tax purposes, and valuations were expected to increase three- to fourfold. (Taxes were minimal by current standards. In 1954, a typical cottage lot off the water was valued at $20 for taxation purposes and the cottage at $1,280. In 2008, that lot and cottage is valued at $62,100. The land for a waterfront cottage was valued at $310 and the cottage at $1,640. In 2008, lot and cottage is valued at $142,500.) A new fire siren was obtained from Freeport to be installed on the roof of the Community House. In 1959, after the Zarbock cottage burned, $1,700 was spent for fire equipment.

In 1957, 120 calls were made from a mobile phone, powered by a battery on the Jeep that George Hatch had brought to the island. His daughter Cynthia operated it as a summer business. Calls were twenty-five cents each and could be made between 8:30 a.m. and 9:00 p.m. For an incoming call, the Jeep was driven to the cottager's door. In the 1960s, when the Jeep was no longer available, telephone service ended.

Also in the 1960s, propane gas for lighting and cooking became widespread, and dissatisfaction was expressed over the way the contract was handled for lighting the thirty-three lamps

Courtesy of Dean L. Lunt
The new Community House opened for island use in 1920.

and streetlights in operation under the auspices of the village corporation. In 1961, the Freeport appropriation for island needs was $3,000. In 1964, the by-laws were amended to prohibit motor vehicles on the island without the approval of the Board of Overseers. Vehicles already on the island were grandfathered.

Store problems were a major topic at the 1966 Annual Meeting. The owners at the time were Eugene Smoker and the late Don Roberts, but the store had been run since 1958 by the Rev. Scotty Campbell, and he was increasingly less willing to continue to do so. The hope was expressed that someone could be found to run the store for the next year, but it was acknowledged that this was not the village corporation's problem, inasmuch as it did not own property. The absence of a solution led to a Special Meeting on August 20 with 41 voters present. The business of the meeting was to amend the island charter—which would require state legislation—so that the corporation could acquire and disburse real and personal property. The intent was perhaps twofold: First, it was to formalize what had been the fact for decades—that it would be legal for the corporation to own the island docks, roads and Community House that it controlled. But second, and the real motivating force as quickly became clear, was to authorize the corporation to purchase the store and related property, to repair it, and to pay the associated taxes and insurance costs. Keeping the store in operation would become a corporation undertaking. The proposals were approved and the corporation assumed new responsibilities that would increase its financial obligations and broaden its island involvements.

In 1968, Board of Overseers chairman Ingham Baker's report noted a number of issues facing the island. These included another Freeport reassessment of cottages, leaving islanders "shocked, stunned or angered" by increases, inequities, and errors. A truck was needed now that islanders, in effect, owned the store and post office.

Environmental concerns began to appear on state and local radar screens. During the year an islander had been arrested and fined for dumping garbage in the bay. In response, Roger Leland bought a gas incinerator from superintendent Lilly Brewer who, it turned out, was agent for two makers. Arthur Silver prepared a comprehensive survey on gas incinerators. Most, he discovered, were of commercial size, too large for use by islanders. So some islanders, it was noted, were burying their garbage—for the raccoons to dig up! In 1969 island income was $6,639 and expenditures were $4,492, with the largest single item being $1,000 to Lilly Brewer as island superintendent.

Despite the still relatively small budgets, the pressure grew to find a different approach to meet island financial needs. Both sides were increasingly cognizant of the uncertainties inherent in islanders coming annually to the town seeking funding. Neither side could plan ahead, one side not knowing what would be requested, and the other, what could/would be appropriated. Turnover on the committees complicated the issues. This year's group might not wish to be bound by understandings reached with last year's group. The problem was exacerbated by the perception amongst Freeporters that the islanders with their vacation cottages were not only from away, but were also well-to-do. Roger Leland recalls that at one meeting with town officials regarding appropriations, he was essentially told: "Mr. Leland, it is only fair to warn you in advance that you are not among friends."

While steadily growing, the island budget remained below $10,000 until 1976, when the Freeport council authorized $14,500 for Bustins. During the island's Annual Meeting that August, expenditures of $23,500 were authorized, including $4,000 for a new island truck and $10,000 toward the cost of building the new island garage. For the year ending May 31, 1979, authorized expenditures amounted to $22,222, including $11,000 for dock repair.

In response to the growing budget, chairman Ken Roberts at the 1980 Annual Meeting warned of two problems affecting island life: government regulation and inflation. He urged islanders to "resist regulation from the outside when possible" and, when necessary, to "accept the responsibility of self-regulation whenever possible." He advised islanders to minimize the effects of inflation by maintaining island property to avoid expensive repairs, and to volunteer for various boards and committees.

What caused such increases in the money needed to run the island's business? Surely inflation, the growing complexity and expense of services provided, and new obligations to meet rising expectations of the islanders were all significant factors. Archie's subsidy continued to rise. Repairs to docks and gravel for road maintenance became more expensive. Removing trash was expensive as people bought newer furnishings and the older furniture needed to be discarded. The village corporation now owned property, a store and post office, and vehicles—which required maintenance and insurance.

A list of projected capital improvement projects covering the years 1975 to 1979 was presented to Freeport. It included a new 30-foot-by-30-foot utility building to house island vehicles and equipment ($30,000), a new float at the Public Dock ($6,000) and a new tractor ($6,000). The present "familiar gray tractor" was twenty years old, the overseers explained, "and might die from old age and winter exposure by 1979." This is, of course, the same "familiar gray tractor" that remained in use almost to the century's end. New committees were appointed, such as the one charged with writing a Shoreland Zoning Ordinance. This committee met frequently and travel expenses needed to be paid. The numbers of islanders willing to volunteer to do island work was declining and work had to be hired out. The cost of doing business was on the rise.

Courtesy of Dean L. Lunt

A Bustins Island fire truck, 2007, just purchased from North Yarmouth.

F. Benjamin Carr

Throughout this period island valuations and taxes increased rapidly. This prompted Leland, in a letter to islanders dated July 28, 1974, to suggest separation from Freeport to which they were paying two to three times more in taxes than was being returned in services. He suggested that the island would be "substantially ahead by having the sole authority to tax itself and, in that manner, be a completely separate entity from Freeport." To the question of whether we should try to get back more money from Freeport, his succinct answer was that the "Island does not need this money." He thought it would be better for the Village Corporation on behalf of the islanders to establish its own sinking fund—$2,000 to $3,000 per year. He felt that Freeport would not object to such an arrangement since island tax monies were small in the overall Freeport picture and, furthermore, Freeport hardly wanted an "unhappy colony." He closed the letter by invoking the time-hallowed rallying cry about the unfairness of taxation without representation, and by informing islanders that he would present a motion embodying these views at the Annual Meeting the next week. He did so, with his customary persuasiveness, and the motion passed by a 46–1 vote.

One tangible result of Leland's secession proposal was a study, prepared at the behest of islanders by Tim Baker, himself an islander. In Baker's *A Study of Bustins Island: Whether to Become an Independent Town* (1975), he evaluated the effect of revaluations, and compared taxes paid by islanders to Freeport with appropriations from Freeport to Bustins. He noted that as a result of revaluation, Bustins' taxes in 1975 had increased 46 percent compared to 1968. Using figures obtained from the town manager, the taxes paid by islanders to Freeport had increased from $7,943 in 1967 to $26,015 in 1975, at which time Bustins islanders were judged to be paying 2.5 percent of the total Freeport tax bill. For Baker this figure reflected the high value of coastal property and was typical of "all property revaluations up and down the Maine coast." Appropriations from Freeport were also rising. From the $2,500 to $3,000 range that had persisted through the late 1960s, figures that represented from one-quarter to one-third of the tax monies paid in, the figure rose to $15,000 in 1975. This amounted to a 57 percent return. He saw few reasons for pursuing independence from Freeport; he foresaw the tax burden on owners doubling if the island became the Town of Bustins Island.

Baker summarized his reasons for continuing the village corporation form of government: lower taxes, direct participation in political affairs by nonresident seasonal islanders, the absence of an established infrastructure for self-government on a year-round basis, and a current healthy relationship with Freeport.

"The rationale for the existence of the BIVC is just as strong today as it was when it was chartered in 1913," he said.

Baker's research cooled the ardor of those islanders who, angry at increasing valuations and property taxes, thought independence a viable option. But it also provided fodder for those of us who saw the need for an established and predictable formula for determining appropriations to the island. In 1981, the suggestion was made at the Annual Meeting that island leaders negotiate with the Freeport Town Council for the return of that portion of our taxes allocated to education. This was a straw in the wind. The next year, with expenditures of $34,600 authorized for the fiscal year ending May 31, 1982, a request was presented for appointment of a committee to study the relationship between the village corporation and the town of Freeport. Nothing much came of this. By 1983, expenditures had risen to $38,800, and islanders still had no firm understanding what level of funding to expect from Freeport. It was time for change—time to find a way for island and town to reach an understanding on finances that would provide each a basis for greater predictability regarding expectations, as well as greater stability in the financial relationship between the two entities.

Impetus for reaching such a new understanding was provided by several islanders, including Jiffy Drew, Roger Leland, Bob Rudolph, and Len Larrabee. The idea wasn't entirely new. In February 1969, Leland was smarting following an unhappy meeting with the Freeport Finance Committee, according to a letter from overseer Bob Clark to overseers Ingham Baker and A. B. LaFleur in the middle of the electrification controversy. Many on the Finance Committee, wrote Bob Clark, conveying Leland's sense, "did not know of the BIVC's existence." He agreed with Leland that it was time to go to the Maine Legislature seeking a change in the Bustins Enabling Act to force Freeport to return an established portion of the taxes it collected from Bustins. Though emotions were strong and pointed, they resulted in no action.

In 1973, Charlie Thomas, chairman of the board, reported on his conversation with Freeport town manager Bruce Benway on July 16. In that conversation Benway reminded Thomas that reassessment was imminent, and recommended that islanders wait for this to be completed before establishing "a fixed percentage return to the island." It is in this direction "that future discussions should lead," he counseled.

This was the beginning of what would, upon culmination more than a decade later, mark a major change in how the island governance is funded and in how the village corporation and the town of Freeport do business.

As the 1980s began, the Freeport assessor completed yet another reassessment of island cottages and their taxes. When the results became known, many islanders were again up in arms, feeling they were treated unfairly in light of other Freeport assessments. This is the perennial complaint of islanders who point to their small old cottages used only seasonally and to the minimal services they require and receive. Shortly thereafter, Bob Rudolph was elected an overseer. Amidst the reassessment furor of the moment, he went to board chairman Jiffy Drew with what he considered the three options open to the islanders: They could go to the Freeport assessor as individuals seeking redress and be turned down one by one. They could go as a group in a class action suit that would presume a unanimity that did not in fact exist. Or they could amend the village corporation charter to incorporate a provision providing return of a fixed percentage of tax monies to the islanders based on the paucity of services provided by the town. This latter would require both legal representation in negotiations with Freeport and then legislation at the state level to amend the 1913 charter. Drew had some concerns about the repercussions of seeking a fixed-percentage return and about the magnitude of the undertaking. David Pease, clerk of the Board of Overseers, thought it a good idea. Lawyer Leland was also supportive, while Bill Cooper, an overseer, felt it would be very difficult to obtain the needed legislation. The idea was not discarded, but neither for the moment was it pursued.

The idea of a fixed-percentage return was given new life when it was presented at the 1983 Annual Meeting. Rudolph presented the same options that he had earlier discussed with Drew, and he favored seeking a fixed-percentage return. He recalls telling the assembled voters that on his own, not as a board member, "I will hire a local attorney to look into the matter" of getting legislation passed leading to fixed-percentage reimbursements. He said that he would accept contributions to offset the costs of this investigation. The first check came from Jan Eckel. A lawyer, recommended by Freeport attorney Paul Powers who was still island counsel at the time, was hired to explore the possibilities.

Sometime earlier the custom had begun of inviting the Freeport Town Council members and other officials to an annual reception and potluck supper on the island, usually in August. Sometimes this gathering was held at an island cottage; at other times it took place in the Community House. It gave island and town office holders and officials the opportunity to meet informally, enjoy a meal together, and share concerns and plans for the future. Of course it also provided the opportunity for town officials to see Bustins firsthand. At the get-together in August 1983, following the Annual Meeting, Drew raised the issue of appropriations. Couldn't we do something to improve the budgeting process, he wondered, perhaps even consider the establishment of a percentage of Bustins tax monies to be returned to the village corporation for the purpose of paying for island expenses?

Spurred on by the initiatives being undertaken by the islanders, a discourse began between islanders, the Freeport Town Council, and newly arrived town manager Dale Olmstead. On Bustins, a Tax Equity Committee was established with Bob Rudolph as chairperson and members including Fred Bohen, Drew, Fred Hohn, Kitchin, Len Larrabee, Leland, John Leyden, and David Pease. These island representatives made serious commitments to attend the meetings of the Freeport Town Council. Often they gathered at David Pease's home in Cumberland beforehand and then went to the meetings together. But from each, time on the highway and juggling of schedules was required. For instance, Bob Rudolph drove up from Massachusetts and would then drive back home after the meeting. Len Larrabee would usually fly to Portland after a day in his New York City law office, change into khaki pants and a sweater at the Portland airport, and meet with David, Bob, and John Leyden, who came from Hebron where he was headmaster of Hebron Academy. Len would overnight at his daughter's home before rising early to take the first flight back to New York to be in his office by 9:00 a.m. John would drive back to Hebron.

The initial meetings were marked by considerable uncertainty. Councilman David Coffin, owner with his brother of what is now the Harraseeket Lunch and its lobster business, was not particularly well disposed toward the Bustins people or their proposals. He had been involved in run-ins with Bud Nickerson and Bob Rudolph at various times over moorings and anchorages.

Beyond personalities, the issues involved were themselves complex. For instance, what services would Freeport be responsible for? Would Freeport continue to be responsible for medical and other emergency services? What about trash removal and provision of dock space for the *Marie L.*? Her presence interfered, according to the Coffins, with the needed access to their slips by the fishing boats doing business with them. And of course, what percentage would satisfy islanders and not outrage townsfolk?

In November 1983, David Coffin left the council, and the atmosphere and dynamics of the meetings quickly changed. Councilwoman Vaughndella Curtis was sympathetic to the evolving plan. So was new councilman John Nelson, a good friend of the Wally and Jerry Baker families, Freeport residents with deep Bustins roots. Nelson visited Bustins frequently. Another new councilwoman, Barbara McGiveran, seemed to have neutral feelings toward Bustins. The new chairman of the council, Hugh Phelps, was sensible in his approach. He saw the benefits to both Freeport and Bustins of altering the long-standing budget process and declared himself ready to consider change.

Early in 1984, Len Larrabee, with input from Bob Rudolph, prepared a lengthy position paper for presentation to the Town Council. In its preparation, the tax structure of Squirrel Island, a village corporation near Boothbay Harbor but paying taxes to Southport, was examined. The needs of Bustins Island were projected over the next years. Necessary operating funds were augmented by figures representing minimum capital needs and for a contingency reserve. The paper concluded by advocating a percentage return to Bustins in the range of 70 percent to 75 percent. Rudolph remembers presenting two arguments to the council. "No one from Bustins Island attends local schools, and so we shouldn't have to pay such high taxes," he argued.

"L.L. Bean doesn't send kids to school, either," town manager Dale Olmstead responded, "but they still pay taxes, including those portions which support public education."

That torpedoed Rudolph's first argument. His second was perhaps more persuasive.

"If I were in your shoes and making a presentation to a town meeting in February when they considered more teachers for education and a dock on Bustins for Massachusetts people," he remembers saying, "you've got a problem. I've got the solution: return our money and you are relieved of supporting Bustins."

Henceforth, both sides shared basic agreements. Islanders, councilmen and Olmstead agreed on the general concepts. Everyone recognized the advantages to each of a fixed-percentage return of tax dollars that would eliminate the annual sparring contest over the request by islanders for funds. Such an agreement would save time and lessen the opportunities for the rise of antagonisms, and would put an end to Freeport's responsibilities for major capital projects or assistance following catastrophic damages on Bustins, such as docks being destroyed in hurricanes. The islanders, for their part, would now be free to plan their spending in accordance with their own priorities, consistent with the concept of village corporations.

Quickly it became clear that no support existed for the suggested 70 to 75 percent return. The Bustins team was soon advised that four council members, a majority of the seven-member council, would support a 60 percent return, but that to expect more would be futile.

The Bustins team accepted that figure. Rudolph rented a conference room in a Boston office building, and Larrabee flew in from New York. They worked and reworked a final draft to be presented to the Freeport Town Council, as well as materials to be presented to both the islanders at their Annual Meeting in August and to the Maine Legislature, where an amendment was needed to the 1913 Enabling Act that created the Bustins Island Village Corporation. Larrabee did the majority of the work on these documents, consulting as needed with both Leland and a legal adviser in Maine.

On July 9, a notice was posted on the island outlining the agreement reached with Freeport. On it were listed the pros and cons of such an agreement, the suggestion of $40,200 as the sum Bustins might receive from the $67,000 paid Freeport in 1983 taxes, and strong emphasis on the significance of the "irrevocable step" being proposed. Informational meetings were held on July 22 and 29, with the proposal set for a vote in early August.

At the August 1984 Annual Meeting, voters were presented with four resolutions. The first directed Freeport to annually pay Bustins a sum equal to 60 percent of all real estate and personal property taxes collected from Bustins, in return for which Freeport would be relieved of the duty to build, repair, and maintain roads, etc. The second would give the village corporation borrowing authority so that it could borrow money as needed to fund municipal services. The third would eliminate any ceiling on self-assessment and any indebtedness that the village corporation might incur. Finally, and not part of the charter amendments, it was proposed that the Board of Overseers be given authority to work with the Freeport Town Council to get these amendments passed by the state legislature.

The proposals passed overwhelmingly.

In October 1984, the Freeport Town Council formally approved the proposal by a 5–2 vote, and both parties entered an agreement.

Freeport's representative in the legislature, James Mitchell, introduced the necessary legislation. The bill was passed and signed into law by Gov. Joseph Brennan on May 23, 1985.

One quirk to the legislative approval was that it required a revote by the islanders and provision for absentee ballots. Pease, as clerk of the village corporation, carefully supervised implementation of the absentee ballot provisions, but they were never used. At the 1985 Annual Meeting, islanders again approved the charter amendments, this time 68–1.

Several unanticipated events were sandwiched in around this radical new—for Bustins—financial reality. While awaiting legislative approval of the agreement, two docks on the island were lost to storms. The agreement contained no emergency provisions for the interim period between formal agreement and implementation through the amended charter. Bob Rudolph went back to the Freeport town manager acknowledging that the island was in trouble and needed help. Bob remembers the reassurance Olmstead offered.

"Don't worry," Bob remembers him saying. "I know the town will come up with what you need." Olmstead was as good as his word.

Shortly after the amendments to the charter were put in place, all of Freeport—with the exception of Bustins Island—was reassessed. Consequently the tax rate was lowered to balance somewhat the increased valuations. Since Bustins valuations had not changed, the taxes it paid decreased significantly, resulting in an unexpected dip in revenues to the village corporation. A number of islanders responded to the board's appeal for contributions and the obstacle was surmounted. Soon Bustins assessments were increased, ending the shortfall. Since then, in the absence of any major catastrophes, the agreement has worked well. It stands as a tribute to those from island and town whose persistent efforts made it happen—and it also provides a little buffering from the encroaching main.

When it became evident that an agreement with Freeport would be reached, Larrabee took the lead in urging the establishment of the Catastrophe and Special Capital Outlays Fund to provide financial resources in the event of unexpected or major needs.

Voters agreed to transfer $27,511 to the fund in 1986. In 1987, the fund grew to $48,124, and by 1991, to $82,500. In 1993, it reached $100,000. In the next years it would increase to more than $140,000 before settling back to a figure below $100,000. Periodically islanders debate how much should be in it and what kind of capital outlays might legitimately be drawn from it.

As the new century began, the fund stood at $84,000. An article presented to islanders in 1999 was passed after heated debate, an article that helps safeguard the fund by requiring a two-thirds vote—rather than a simple majority—to withdraw from it.

Budgets have continued to mushroom over the years. For a time the island seemed to have more money than it knew what to do with. Some thought was given to returning a portion of the tax monies to those who had paid the taxes in the first place. This groundswell, appealing in concept, never went far; it was feared that Freeport would find a way of abrogating the agreement when such disposition of tax monies became public knowledge. It didn't take long for us to learn how to disburse all the money coming to us. The combination of the increasing costs of governance and the expenditures we authorized at the annual meetings—along with a decline in volunteerism—quickly eliminated any excess funds burning holes in the village corporation's pockets.

A budget of $62,000 was approved for the 1992 fiscal year. Anticipated revenues for the next year were $68,237, which included $66,837 from Freeport—a far cry from the $5,000 subsidy received just twenty years earlier.

In 2003, the budget adopted topped $203,000; of this amount nearly $160,000 came from Freeport as a result of the 60 percent agreement. Surely the times had changed. Surely islanders should be grateful each day for the foresight and determination of those who helped establish the 60 percent agreement.

Chapter Eight

Regulation Comes to Bustins

MAINE islands, whether summer or year-round, share many similar challenges and pressures today. They are connected to the mainland by a profusion of ties and obligations unknown to earlier generations, and they feel the encroachment of state government in ways unimagined fifty years ago. Bustins is no exception. The impact of rules and regulations passed in Augusta requires more and more of islanders to formulate policies and regulations and then administer and enforce those rules to the state's satisfaction. If Bustins folk can remember a time "when town and state pretended we didn't exist, and we pretended they didn't exist," that time is no more.

The first shot across our bow occurred in the early 1970s after mandatory shoreline zoning became a state priority. This zoning pertained to all land within 250 feet of the water on freshwater lakes and ponds inland as well as within 250 feet of the high-water mark along the coast. In particular, as coastal communities grew and developers sought building sites, traditional methods of dealing with wastewater, maintaining the purity of well water, and development needed scrutiny.

Increasingly, it became clear to many that unregulated development was not in the best interests of the environment or the coastal communities that seemed loath or unable to protect their own shorelands. Consequently, the state passed a generic Shoreland Zoning Ordinance to maintain what it considered safe conditions along waterfronts, to preserve beauty, prevent pollution, and protect wildlife habitats. The ordinance took effect in the summer of 1973 for all coastal communities that had not developed their own ordinances by that time. Such ordinances, to be modeled on the state ordinance and submitted for state approval, could be stricter but not more lenient than the state ordinance. Eventually, the deadline for adoption was pushed out to 1974.

Bustins Island was included in the mandate from the state. This realization came as somewhat of a shock to us. We, not unlike many Maine communities, had long operated under a philosophy of laissez-faire in matters of how we used our land and how we expected to be governed by our Board of Overseers. "That government is best which governs least" expressed our general sentiment.

In any event, at the 1973 Annual Meeting, with the state deadline less than a year away, a committee was appointed to create a Bustins Island zoning ordinance that would pass state muster and simultaneously protect the prevailing interests of islanders. Appointed chairman was Roger Leland, the Massachusetts lawyer who had been very active in island issues and governance for years. Rod Allard, my wife, Marilyn, David Pease, and Al Spalding completed the committee.

Only one committee meeting took place on the island in the summer of 1974. The brief time between the Annual Meeting and Labor Day, when islanders traditionally close their cottages, precluded more than an organizational meeting. But during the off-season, a succession of meetings took place. Committee members were scattered from Massachusetts to New Hampshire to Washington County, Maine, so Valle's Restaurant in Kittery was selected as the meeting spot. Kittery was roughly a five-hour drive from our home Down East. Committee members convened in late afternoon, worked through supper and into the evening. They either drove home during the late-night hours or spent the night and made the drive home in the morning.

Initially, the committee looked at ordinances established by other states, notably Massachusetts and New Hampshire. Later they tackled the Maine ordinance, working to see how Bustins fit with a shoreland zoning plan intended primarily for mainland communities. As they began to formulate a proposed ordinance, in part by tailoring the state ordinance to fit on the island, some articles of the state ordinance were clearly inappropriate. It seemed unlikely, for instance, that anyone would propose establishing a trailer park on our shorefront land. Other articles in the state ordinance were kept simply as evidence that they had not been ignored. A Housing and Urban Development article was initially included, for instance, only to be excised as irrelevant some years later. Still other articles were amended to affirm that we would have no inns or commercial establishments.

A primary accomplishment of the committee was the creation of a Resource Protection District in the middle of the island where few cottages existed and where most owners had one or more woodlots that generally passed from generation to generation. As part of the new zoning ordinance, it was proposed that a large number of interior lots be designated for inclusion in the Resource Protection District. The trees could be used for firewood, but no structures could be built on them. Some owners saw the inclusion of their woodlots in a protection area as an infringement on their individual rights since they would no longer be able to use their woodlots as they might choose. To make this restriction more palatable, Freeport officials agreed to reduce taxes on lots that were no longer buildable. The purpose of this Resource Protection District was, of course, to establish and protect an area believed to be critical to the underground lens of water creating the island's water supply. Trees protected the ground beneath them and water from rain or snow had a chance to sink in and enhance the island's water table. If, as had been claimed by islanders quoted nearly a century earlier in *Glimpses of Portland and Casco Bay, Maine*, Bustins water was "equal to the celebrated Poland Spring water," the Resource Protection District would help preserve that purity. At the same time, by prohibiting cottage construction within its boundaries, it effectively reduced pressure on the available water supply over the long run.

While a few families chose to retain their prerogative to sell their lots as house lots at some future date, most islanders acquiesced for what they saw as the common welfare. Since then the few requests to remove lots from the protected area have been rebuffed at the island level, and no further legal action has been taken.

Leland's leadership was critical to the success of the committee's efforts that ultimately led to the Zoning Ordinance of the Bustins Island Village Corporation of Bustins Island, Maine. Lots of hearings preceded the Annual Meeting vote on July 1, 1975. Lots of questions were asked and lots of questions answered. When the vote finally came, one strong voice rose in opposition: Bill Clark. Clark said that if we had to have a zoning code, this was a good one, but he didn't really want any darn bill at all. The ordinance took effect on September 1, 1975. After living with the ordinance for a quarter-century, most islanders feel that the island is better off, despite the loss of some property rights. In addition, the island now has management and enforcement mechanisms that never existed before.

Mechanisms for implementation and enforcement are integral to the long-term success of any ordinance. We needed a mechanism for seeking variances from the established usage for our land; an appeal process should we be denied variances; a means of oversight to assure that what the ordinance required was in fact being observed. From these needs arose boards and officers, taken for granted in 2000, but newly established and often honored more in the breach than the observance in 1975.

The Planning Board emerged as the primary repository for all matters pertaining to shoreland zoning and zoning in general. The board has been fortunate to have had strong leadership throughout its existence. Leland was its first chairman, followed by Wally Baker, Robbie Boone, John Garfield, and Bill Cooper. The board undertook a variety of initiatives to educate islanders about the new ordinance and to create a uniform process for anyone planning to build, renovate, or extend cottages and facilities. It also worked to conserve island resources and to keep the island and our ordinance in conformity with changes at the state level as shoreland zoning evolved.

The ordinance established a permitting process for us to use if we were building afresh or simply adding a porch, a room or a shed. Information concerning plumbing was especially crucial. More and more cottagers were forsaking outhouses and rain barrels to install inside bathrooms and flush toilets with requisite septic tanks to be tucked in somewhere on a small lot located along the waterfront and in close proximity, perhaps, to wells owned by neighbors. Handling requests in such a way as to preserve water purity, as well as long-standing friendships, became a priority. New wells had to be at least 75 feet from septic tanks, and vice versa. This was not easy to accomplish with many Bustins lots being but 66 by 100 feet.

At the 1980 Annual Meeting, Leland promised to work for "reasonable" steps and laws. He recognized the limitations of our island with its thin soil and limited space. Solutions to problems of both gray and black waste matter would be based on "reasonableness and financial practicability." He would frequently describe the Planning Board's approach to issues as embodying a "yes, if" rather than a "no, because" philosophy.

Meanwhile, enforcement responsibility was vested in a code enforcement officer appointed by the board to ensure that a building permit from the Town of Freeport was obtained and displayed, that what was being built was consistent with what had been approved, and especially that complicated and expensive systems for waste disposal met all regulations. The code enforcement officer's task is not an easy one.

The zoning issues and requirements are compounded by the closeness of so many projects to the rocky edge of Casco Bay and its salt water. A primary island resource, not well understood but requiring unceasing vigilance, is the supply of fresh water. Once it was thought that Bustins water came through underground channels from the mountains to our west. Today we realize that our water comes entirely from precipitation. This water, whether referred to as groundwater or surface water, all has the same origin, and because much of it finds its way to the aquifer that underlies the island, the island is said to have a "single-source aquifer." The aquifer consists of fresh water that floats on the salt water that permeates the rock deep below the island. Since salt water is 1.025 times heavier than fresh water, it stays below, and the fresh water lies atop in what would appear as a lens if we could see it in cross section. This lens is deep and rounded in the middle below the island; it is but a sliver where it meets the sea at the island's edge. The rule-of-thumb suggests that on an island greater than five acres, the depth of the lens is generally forty times the height of the island's groundwater level above the seawater level. If the groundwater level on Bustins is 15 feet above mean sea level, the lens at its center might be 600 feet deep.

But this lens is very fragile. It depends on adequate penetrable island surface for its well-being. The more the island is built up, the more the ground is covered with homes and other structures, the less the penetrable surface that remains. Gradually, without sufficient surface to allow for recharging the aquifer, our water supply would dry up. The Resource Protection District, properly maintained, will ensure that sufficient surface is left to maintain the aquifer. But an aquifer can be contaminated, particularly if it decreases in size/volume to the point that salt water penetrates it at its sliver-thin edges or if it is contaminated from septic systems and the like.

The increasing number of deep wells being drilled on the island presents a potential threat to the island's freshwater supply. On several occasions following creation of the zoning ordinance, well-drilling rigs were barged to the island off-season to drill wells for islanders. Starting in 1981, some forty such deep wells were drilled. Most were operated by electricity rather than deep-well hand pumps, and it was widely suspected that such systems encouraged more water use, especially when the systems were connected, as most were, to inside plumbing.

To facilitate better decision making, a water study was commissioned. Gerber Associates, a local firm experienced in island water issues, produced The Bustins Island Ground Water Survey, completed in 1991, that surveyed well depths, flow rates, types of pumps, and usage for eighty-seven island wells. Rain barrel usage was also incorporated. In addition, the survey assessed average annual water replenishment based on the average inches of rainfall over the island's 138 acres. The results of this survey provided an assessment of our overall water usage as well as an idea of how rapidly water supplies replenished.

While this survey used a nonspecific computer model to interpret data from on-site observation, thereby giving detractors the occasion to dismiss it, the fact remains that it was the best assessment of our situation then available. New and updated information is now being amassed so that, using current models, we can make a new assessment of our water supply.

With a part-time governing Board of Overseers, not all of whom live in Maine, Bustins is sometimes remiss in meeting less-obvious state obligations and deadlines. Such was the case in 1998 when it was discovered that the island needed a comprehensive plan. Under a 1971 Maine statute, all Maine communities were required to prepare comprehensive plans incorporating existing studies and ordinances as well as an assessment of the community's historic, archaeological, and scenic resources. The self-examination involved in preparing such a comprehensive plan, the "benchmark" information such a process provides, and the guidance such a plan makes available for the future could be invaluable to the village corporation, island committees and organizations, and anyone seeking to reflect on the island and its future.

Consequently, by the authority embodied in its own zoning ordinance, the Planning Board in September 1998 chartered a Comprehensive Plan Steering Committee and appointed Erica Morgan as chairperson. She in turn recruited me as cochairman. This comprehensive plan, "formulated with the assistance of the island's residents, its governmental bodies and the various island community organizations, would describe Bustins and its community today, depict what these might be like in the future, and provide guidance for how this vision might be attained. The plan would be consistent with the requirements of the Bustins Zoning Ordinance, guided by the recommendations of the Maine Growth Management statute (1988), and would reflect the uniqueness of Bustins Island as a small summer community."

Over the next two-plus years the Comprehensive Plan gradually took shape. Slowly the voluminous material we collected by research, questionnaire, interview, and casual conversation amongst islanders was assessed, condensed, and organized by a steering committee working not only during the summer months but also over the winter. These workers represented as many island constituencies as possible: old-timers and newcomers, owners and renters, boat owners and ferry riders, youth and elderly, and all sides of the island. Eventually, the report *Bustins*

F. Benjamin Carr

Today and Tomorrow: A Foundation for Island Planning was presented at the annual meeting in 2001 and approved.

The Planning Board continues to be an integral and productive committee. It oversees the surveying of island roads and resolves issues when it is discovered that the dirt roads aren't located just where the original surveys indicate they should be. It is contracting for a new Global Positioning System–based mapping of island lot boundaries and other salient information. Every year it proposes needed changes to update ordinances and keep them current with changes in state mandates. Ongoing efforts focus on assuring that the ordinance is both internally self-consistent and consistently applied, and that the various processes it mandates are user-friendly for a summer island community with a well-established preference for permitting its cottagers to do pretty much what they wish on their properties. The ordinance and pertinent application forms and procedures are now available online. Over the quarter-century of its existence, the board has been fortunate in the quality of its members and leadership, in its ability to reach viable decisions on the manifold issues that have come before it, and in its willingness to enforce those decisions reached. It has earned the trust—admittedly, sometimes grudging—of islanders who philosophically oppose the increasing presence of "government" in their island affairs but who have become only too aware of "the encroaching main."

Chapter Nine

Bustins Buys a Boat

IN 1999, the Bustins Island Village Corporation asked voters if they would approve spending up to $180,000 to purchase and equip a ferry for the run from Freeport to Bustins. If approved, it would mark the beginning of yet another new journey for Bustins islanders, and another one into uncharted waters.

Considerable transportation history preceded this new venture, but it was Archie Ross's retirement in 1996 that actually spurred it. As the 1997 season approached, islanders waited for announcement of the new service. We wondered whether the new captain would let us off at docks closer to our cottages. We wondered whether he would help us load suitcases, cartons, animals, children, and plants when we arrived at the South Freeport dock just minutes before scheduled departure and whether he would then wait while we drove up to the Soule School to park. Would he soothe the ruffled feathers of those who arrived early and were waiting impatiently, counting every waiting minute as wasted island time?

The Ferry Boat Committee was responsible for finding new service. The committee initially included Sue Spalding, Erica Morgan, Len Larrabee, Jiffy Drew, and Kevin Hughes. Questions were prepared for potential captains, knowing they must mesh with a somewhat demanding, somewhat eccentric island family. Tom Ring of South Freeport was interested in providing service with the *Atlantic Seal* in conjunction with his sightseeing tours to Eagle Island. Others also showed interest,

Courtesy of Dean L. Lunt
The Lilly B. *crossing Casco Bay on its return run to South Freeport in* 2007.

including the Carrier family, who proposed doing business as the Carrier Freight and Delivery service. Amongst the others was Doug Reepmeyer, a young man from the Boothbay area.

The interviews were completed, the committee conferred, and the announcement was made: We would be served by the *Maranbo II* from Boothbay Harbor with Captain Reepmeyer at the wheel. For $15,000, Reepmeyer leased the *Maranbo II* for the summer season from her owners, the Campbells, who had used her on the Squirrel Island run and for charters. The total summer subsidy would be $28,000, including boat lease and salary, and would remain the same for 1998. The wooden *Maranbo II* was an older boat, slightly larger than the *Marie L.*, and seemed to fit our vision of what our ferry should look like. Reepmeyer was young, as was Archie when he took the job, and worked hard to meet the expectations of the committee, now called the Boat Advisory Committee. By this time the members were Dave Stager, Lois Dennett, Charlie Johnson, Nat Molloy, and Sue Spalding. Its mission was "to ease the transition from the old to the new ferry system" and "to ensure the success of the Bustins Island Ferry Service for both the Island and the boat operator."

Despite the occasional—and inevitable—tensions and problems inherent in any new enterprise, the arrangement seemed a satisfactory one, and Reepmeyer was hired again for 1998. It appeared that a long-term relationship might be in the making. Consequently the committee was shocked to hear from Reepmeyer in August of 1998 that the *Maranbo II* could not pass Coast Guard safety requirements. These included the need for three sistered frames, as well as a newly required fire-fighting system, total cost $6,000 to $10,000. The boat's owners were not prepared make that kind of investment.

The committee hoped that somehow both *Maranbo II* and Reepmeyer would return for 1999, or that at least Reepmeyer would return in another leased boat. Meanwhile, the boat committee reformed as the Boat Service Search Committee. Reepmeyer notified the committee that he wanted to return and was considering buying a boat in South Carolina, toward which he needed $7,000. The board seemed favorably inclined toward this request. Other operators also began to express an interest and new options presented themselves, but after discussions played out, the search committee decided to negotiate a contract extension with Reepmeyer and authorize spending up to $6,000 to bring the *Maranbo II* up to Coast Guard certification standards. However, all this incorrectly presupposed approval by the Campbell family, which, by March decided that they didn't wish to lease their boat after all.

So we were back to square one and the situation appeared dire.

At the March 1999 overseers' meeting, Dave Stager, a new member, proposed two options: the current model, in which a captain ran the service as a private business, or a model in which the island, through the overseers, would manage the service as a nonprofit business. Following extended discussion, the overseers chose option two. They also approved three related items: that a ferry service emergency existed; that $28,000 would be allotted to the Boat Service Search Committee to arrange for and manage boat service; and that the $28,000 would come from the island's fund for emergencies.

By April, Betty Kirkland, island treasurer, was chosen as bookkeeper for the new island ferry enterprise, and another islander, Sandy Colburn, would handle payroll. By May, a lease was finalized with Hilda Dudley of Cape Elizabeth to lease the *Polly-Lin II* for the 1999 summer season at a cost of $16,500. Captain Rick Morse of Edgecomb was hired for the summer.

Meanwhile, the committee also assumed responsibility for more and more aspects of the boat service. Members met with the captain as needed, proceeds from fares and baggage were collected daily for deposit in the bank, the boat manager kept the books, and payrolls were met. An increasing number of people assumed responsibilities that were, for so many years, handled by Archie alone. More and more we realized what an underappreciated giant he had been.

Three years of dealing with boat transportation gave members of the Boat Advisory Committee, as it was once again renamed, perspective. While its original task was simply finding a replacement for Archie, it was actually forced to handle all the crises that arose regarding boat service. And it now served as an intermediary committee between the boat service and islanders, its mission to provide satisfactory ferry service, which is critical to island life. Based on its experience, the committee was convinced change was crucial.

At the June overseers' meeting the committee requested that voters be asked to approve the purchase of an island ferry. The Board of Overseers accepted this request but said that before it agreed to support such an article, it wanted to explore a water

F. Benjamin Carr

Courtesy of Linda Sweatt

The Lilly B. *leaving Bustins Island.*

taxi model, and get solid estimates on the cost of a boat and how it would be financed.

The two months between the meeting of the overseers in June and the Annual Meeting in August were full of research, meetings, and discussion. The pros and cons were discussed on every porch and in front of the old store as islanders waited for the day's mail. Fliers were distributed answering the most frequently asked questions. Public information meetings were held. We were being asked to support by far the largest financial request that had ever appeared on an annual island budget. On the eve of the Annual Meeting, no one knew how the vote would go, but all were sure that the turnout would be large.

On Saturday, August 7, 1999, the Annual Meeting began at the stroke of 9:00 a.m. After handling other business—and after what seemed an endless wait—the boat question was finally introduced.

Dave Stager, chairman of the boat committee, presented the issues. The committee members had seen three basic choices, but ended up with a fourth, he said. The islanders could:

Seek another owner-operator like Archie.

Seek another operator using a leased boat.

Lease a boat and seek to hire a captain for that boat as was currently being done with Rick Morse.

Purchase a boat and hire a captain.

The third option seemed the most harrowing process; the committee had been meeting every other week for the preceding six months—a process the members were unwilling to go through on an annual basis. Captains were available; the missing piece of the puzzle was the boat.

Consequently, after measuring each possibility against the criteria they had adopted—docking constraints in South Freeport arising from pressure from the Coastal Harbors Commission and commercial fishermen, Coast Guard certification, safety, availability, scheduling, and costs—and finding that each fell short, the committee recommended purchasing a boat.

A new boat would have a fifty-year life expectancy, would be paid for in ten years, and then would be available without loan costs for the next forty years. The boat proposed would be a 40-foot Osmond Beal lobster boat hull purchased from H and H Boatworks in Steuben. The bare hull would be finished off by Bradley Simmons of East Boothbay, who would install the engine, steering, mechanical/plumbing/electrical systems, and other needed equipment. Bradley Simmons, it turned out somewhat serendipitously, was Lilly Brewer's grandson and had spent many summers as a boy on Bustins Island.

The issue was on the table. Vigorous debate and discussion ensued, including the introduction by Kevin Hughes of yet another potential option—contracting with Tom Ring, who operated the *Atlantic Seal*, which also generated considerable debate and at times nearly hijacked the meeting.

Janice Knight didn't want to spend $180,000 on the basis of one hour's discussion. Betty Kirkland, acknowledging that we needed a boat, worried about the finances as well as her feeling that "Bustins shouldn't be in the boat business." Charlie Johnson countered that we were already in the boat business and that we wouldn't know much more in another year. Harold Wade delivered his decision, emphasizing the "necessity for permanent, sure service." Erica Morgan felt the new boat offered the "best option for reliable service," that we needed to get to a point where "we have a sure thing." John Garfield said that although we would have higher expenses for ten years, we would then have substantially lower costs indefinitely. To applause he concluded, "To me this is almost like a no-brainer." Robbie Boone felt that "if we don't go now, we just continue to patchwork."

Finally, as the debate continued and veered down new directions, Mike Koleda rose to speak, and his words sharply delineated the direction in which the debate had drifted.

"Seems to me . . . we have a committee that has been charged with looking at every aspect of this problem, has done that, and is now being asked to defend itself against the proposal [hiring Tom Ring] that did not come through the committee, that came in the last 24 or 48 hours which is being debated and defended. . . . procedurally I find it a very uncomfortable situation."

The impact of his words swept through the hall.

Almost immediately the end of the debate was presaged when Charlie Kitchin moved the question. A few others still wanted to speak, but his motion carried and debate ended. A motion for a secret ballot passed and voting ensued. While the ballots were counted, the meeting moved along to the ensuing warrant articles. After a careful count, the results were announced. Of 107 votes cast, eighty-three favored buying a boat, while twenty-four were opposed.

The next nine months were busy ones. Contracts were entered into with both H and H Boatworks for the hull and Simmons for finishing the boat. One of the issues related to contracts. The H and H people were accustomed to using contracts, but a cultural clash between old Maine and the new world occurred when Simmons was given a contract to sign. In it he promised to do his best work, and it included a provision for disposition of materials were he to be injured. Simmons had always worked by handshake and was insulted that anyone would think he would do less than his best work. He refused to sign. Waves of consternation rippled out amongst the island lawyers who lived by contracts and who felt they needed a contract to protect the public monies being committed. The village corporation's new treasurer, John Garfield, remembers writing out a check for $52,000 to the Boatworks during a meeting in October 1999, and pushing it across the table to the island lawyers. The check, it was suggested, would provide some credibility to the request for a signed contract. Meanwhile, Brad showed the contract to his lawyer who told him to sign it—that he would never see a simpler one. Brad signed and that hurdle was crossed.

Naval architect Al Spalding, an islander with forty-five years' experience as a boat designer and known for his classic designs, drew up the plans. He also did all the paperwork and kept up extensive correspondence with the Coast Guard to be sure that the boat met all certification regulations. Caring for these major matters as well as donating any fees for his professional services was a major contribution. So was the contribution by Dave Stager. No one will know the hours he spent ensuring that construction details were carried out in a timely and proper fashion as well as in smoothing ruffled feathers and acting as a sympathetic link between us and the builders. John Garfield devoted much effort and expertise to caring for the financing.

A name was chosen for the new boat. As had been suggested by Marilyn and me right after voters approved the purchase, she would be named the *Lilly B.* after our beloved islander. Many islanders contributed to an "amenities fund" which grew to $4,000 and from which such items as a beautiful compass in honor of Archie, a ship's clock, and other items would be purchased.

On April 22, 2000, the day before Easter, with the temperature in the thirties and a cold rain falling, a group of people gathered at the C and B Marina in East Boothbay where the new ferry hung suspended in the slings of a travel lift. Stager addressed the sodden group, thanking Simmons for his attention and care in finishing the boat. He talked about how the name chosen for the boat was so appropriate.

Finally the long-awaited moment arrived. Maxine, Lilly's daughter, and mother of the builder, christened our boat the *Lilly B.* with a whack of the champagne bottle.

We had a boat and looked forward to it providing us safe and comfortable passage for decades to come as we traveled back and forth between island and mainland.

Chapter 10

My Community, Our Community

THE DAY is just dawning when I turn on the radio at six for the early-morning weather report and news. I listen to familiar voices report on the latest crisis in some city, in Augusta, on the world's battlefields. I hear about violence against this person or that group. And I am grateful for the safety I feel as I lie back against the pillows, listen to the virtuoso performance by the song sparrow in the birch outside, and know that my little island will never be the target for anyone's bombs or violence.

Some people find satisfaction, security, even tranquility in knowing where their personal piece of the world begins and ends. Bustins Island offers me a defined space, a unity. Yes, we have seen controversy among our ranks during the last decades with the electrification vote and other upheavals, but our island has boundaries: one step too far and my feet are wet or I'm up to my knees in oozy mud. The sea provides the buffer between what seems my simple island life and the complexities of life ashore. My island is a little world of its own offering its own topography and flora that I know well, its paths and gravel roads, its medley of smells and its vistas, its varieties of flowers, its successive bounty of berries whose ripening is dictated by the season and its own inner blueprint. And, of course, its people.

Some of my reflections are fantasy, of course. They conveniently ignore certain realities. Wherever human beings gather, issues arise and divide them. Neighbors don't always act exactly as I think neighbors should act. The possibility may even exist,

A Maine Summer Island: The Story of Bustins

Courtesy of Ben Carr

A Fourth of July ham and bean supper at the Community House.

perish the thought, that I don't act exactly as my neighbors think I should act. Some people are always late for the ferry, some people always manage to get their bags into the island truck before others, some ally themselves with this or that clique, some want to hold out land for their children rather than putting it into conservation, some inconvenience others when they tie up the dock excessively with their boats. These are all petty matters, but they do ruffle the placid surface.

The island offers a variety of rhythms, a variety of parameters within which to live life. I am governed day to day by the summer ferry schedule, by the brief opening hours of the post office, whether the tide is rising or falling dictating whether I take the longer or shorter course to South Freeport in my powerboat. Seasons' rhythms provide a larger framework for life as the hours of daylight lengthen or shorten and as days grow warmer or cooler. When do I look for mayflowers or clintonia; when will the full moon rise over Goose? When will the early-morning sunrise be perfectly aligned with the edges of Sow and Pigs, Pettengill, Williams and Sisters islands on a line down to Mere Point to my northeast? When will the ferry be full of excited neighbors arriving for the weekend; when will the island be empty and cottages shuttered? When will the first frost surprise me? In short, the island helps provide refuge, definition, and a rhythm for the world I live in, a world with beginnings and endings, an outer life amongst people and an inner life of the spirit. Being able to encompass beginnings and endings helps make clear the length and breadth of the place for which, and for now, I am steward.

Clearly what an island represents appears as important as what an island is. An island may have as much to do with a state of mind as it does with rocky shores and vegetation, location and topography. We envision a mistiness, an apartness with a touch of romance to it, the hint of a special way of living with its attendant lore and legends. Perhaps an island provides a form of mental and spiritual retreat. An island represents what we dream about, a place where those traditional virtues of freedom and individuality—and neighborliness—stand tall, where one sets one's own schedule for each day. It is large enough not to be claustrophobic and small enough to be known. It is a world of our own, in spite of its many visitors. "Now I guess it's everybody's island," one old-timer lamented about his island. "Doesn't matter, though; your island is always kind of inside you anyway."

Another old-timer shared similar sentiments about life on her island. "No, I was never lonely," she answered the question. "I was alone sometimes—well, people-alone. But not world-alone."

So an island has to do with a state of mind as much as with a particular and distinct landmass. It is a place of retreat for mind and spirit where, perhaps, our dreams can come true.

Integral to my sense of island, along with its being surrounded by water and representing a place of refuge and independence, is "community." As islanders, the phrase "the Bustins community" laces our casual conversation, fills the columns of the *Store Porch*, our island's semiannual newsletter, and appears time and again in the documents emanating from this or that committee. It refers to all of us who love this irregular aggregation of rock projecting from the gray-green sea in Casco Bay. This fact has become more important to us over the past half century. For in the years since World War II America has been characterized by an increasingly mobile and fractious society.

Our community roots grow out of the commingling of the past, the place, and the people. A remembered past, our personal memories, interwoven with the stories of others, with the community's shared memories, seems crucial. We are, after all, in many ways the sum of our memories, of our stories. We are no more than two-dimensional beings without those tales. On Bustins, we are all inheritors of those stories, Bustins stories, and we honor them. If we are third- or fourth- or even fifth-generation islanders, the history and the stories continue part of our very warp and woof.

But even if our families haven't been here that long, we very quickly become possessors of the common past. Virtually every cottage contains a revered and well-thumbed copy of Richardson's *History of Bustins Island*. It is full of history, anecdotes, and photos. Islanders pore over the book, always finding something they had overlooked before. In the process they come to feel familiar with and a part of all that had happened earlier: the old steam ferries that faithfully served the island; the annual Bustins Bust; the evening lamp-lighting as lamps were hung to cast a small circle of light along the roads; the golfing exploits of the old-timers. They read stories about the Smokers and the island store, about Mr. Miller who built the Log Cabin and brought his pony Brownie to the island from Massachusetts each summer, about John Jaynes driving a Model T Ford across the ice to Bustins, about Admiral MacMillan's Camp Wychmere for boys where Cole Porter spent a summer. We pick up all the other little threads. We sit on porches as the sun sinks in the west and retell the old tales: about how

Courtesy of Dean L. Lunt

The post office window today. The post office is open from 9:30 a.m. to 12:30 p.m., six days a week.

Archie lost his ferry, *Victory*, in a storm and how the islanders helped him buy a new boat; how Lew Ward was shingling the old farmhouse and the fog came in so thick he shingled three feet beyond the edge before he knew it; and how Ralph Brewer superintended the reconstruction of the Brainard dock without using any cranes or barges. We learn the Bustins cheer from Camp Wychmere days. that begins "Boom-a-lacka, Cheese-a-lacka, Boom-a-lacka-lah. Bustins! Bustins! Rah-rah-rah!"

The friendships made while playing volleyball or kick the can or flashlight tag as children, the shared experiences of messing about in small boats, exploring adjacent islands and feeling exhilaration when finding our own tie-up ahead of a squall bearing down, are the friendships that mature as we mature, the memories we carry through life. While it is not obligatory to marry another island person—although more than a few do—it

A Maine Summer Island: The Story of Bustins

Roger Leland's dock, 2007. *Courtesy of Dean L. Lunt*

is important to be sure that a mate shares some similar feelings about the island. If the prospective mate feels cooped up on the island, finds the island too small and an outhouse too primitive, finds little in common with other islanders, then a serious decision looms; a choice between two loves, of place and person. For it seems that few people's view of the island changes, very little middle ground exists. Either people love the island or they loathe it. Finding this out before marriage is critical.

Islanders meet a variety of others in the course of life, through jobs, neighborhoods, schools, organizations, and churches, for example, and often these acquaintanceships grow into good friendships. But the enduring friendships, the life friendships, are often the earliest friendships, renewed annually when the island community reconvenes. They are cemented by shared experiences, traditions perpetuated, challenges encountered and overcome, common values held. A special sense of satisfaction comes from

F. Benjamin Carr

knowing that your grandchildren look forward to being with their friends here each summer, and that those playmates are the grandchildren of those who, years ago, were the young friends you waited eagerly to find here each summer.

But those strong roots are sustained not only by a remembered past. Community is nurtured in the present. Bustins is an island whose cottagers, arriving with the enthusiasm that spring nourishes, continue conversations with neighbors as though there had been no ten-month hiatus between sentences. We discover just what we left, with sorrow, the preceding fall—including the roof that needs reshingling, the sill that must be jacked up or replaced, and the puckerbrush that blocks the view and begs to be cut. We know and trust the people we will meet at the dock, on the roads, opening cottages as our summer village reconvenes and doors are unlocked for a new season. We help a neighbor grapple for a mooring and chain lost over the winter. We help—or get help— to start a stubborn lawn mower. We help fix a broken copper water pipe so that a cottage water system will hold pressure. We help remove winter shutters that have protected fragile windows and doors from the wintry blast. We honor privacy, always whistling or calling loudly at least once before climbing the weathered steps to a neighbor's porch. During the season we share in a variety of activities. Some serve on the official boards of the island; some work to maintain the basic fire equipment. Some trim underbrush from roadways and paths. Some volunteer as docents for the Historical Society's summer exhibit. We support the summer Field Day and the bake sales of the cottagers' association, we attend the Fourth of July bean supper and line the road to cheer as fire trucks, Model T Fords, floats and flag-waving islanders slowly parade by in patriotic display. We hold up our colored cards to register our votes at the Annual Meeting in August. A community requires folks who have put down roots, folks who participate and serve, who respect and foster that community.

If we share a past and a present, we also have hopes for the future. We have a sense of ownership in this community. Our motivation to care for a piece of land or an area, whether on an island or the mainland, comes when we have a direct interest in that land, when we see it as enduring and permanent. We have an interest in it for as long as we live, and we envision that our children and grandchildren can continue to enjoy it as we have. So, not without occasional grumbling, we work within the guidelines of the zoning ordinance when we build or renovate, and we are increasingly sensitive to the threats to our environment through pollution. We think about good fire-prevention practices, knowing that fire is one of our most formidable enemies.

None of this is to suggest that challenges never loom, that change never occurs, from the major to the minor. We've had our larger issues, but at the same time, we do need to deal with the occasional unleashed dog bothering other islanders, the party that is too noisy too late at night, youngsters on speedy bicycles startling older folks into the roadside puckerbrush, the planned renovation that has not gone through the approval process and will block a neighbor's view. Tensions stress the relationships between those who want all the comforts of home on Bustins and those who come to distance themselves from those comforts. We do need to deal with differences between neighbors or the occasional island factions that arise over some issue and become shrill and divisive. But somehow in our island community, these challenges—perhaps because we are long-term friends, occasionally despite the fact that we are long-term friends—seem more manageable. The madness of the moment is overcome by community spirit that finally trumps the threats and possible losses growing out of our dissensions.

Amidst the challenges, our island culture has changed as well. The changes from kerosene to propane stoves, from iceboxes to gas refrigerators, from steam- to diesel-powered ferries, from shopping at the island store to going ashore to shop Shaw's, from noisy generators to solar arrays—all these seem less significant than the changes on the mainland that affect the island culture.

Leisure activities have come to the forefront for a great segment of the populace. The availability of inexpensive and fast plane service to all points of the globe eases the pressure to always go to the same summer island, as do employment patterns which find both parents as well as offspring working. Not everyone finds as appealing the quirkiness of island living, with its army of canvas L.L. Bean bags for lugging supplies from the boat to the cottage, the dearth of modern conveniences, the lack of ready-made diversions, and the potential for being cold—or wet—or both—in and out of season. As a result, who comes to the island, how they entertain themselves, and how long they stay is altered.

Mainland regulations also affect the island community as they never have before. Shoreland zoning alters where building can

Courtesy of Ben Carr
The "island vehicle" owned by the Bustins Island Village Corporation is one of the only vehicles on the island.

A Maine Summer Island: The Story of Bustins

occur and how islanders view and use the shoreline. Plumbing codes affect the problems of waste disposal for anyone considering abandoning the old seasonal outhouses. The pollution in Casco Bay changes the quality of shellfish and overharvesting limits the available quantity while at the same time sending the prices soaring. The meteoric rise of real estate taxes has forced some owners to consider selling, and has pushed others to rent their cottages. Cottages that were built for less than one thousand dollars were sold for ten thousand or more dollars twenty-five years ago, for seventy-five thousand dollars a decade ago, and today command prices in six figures. Often, of course, a cottage will be bought by another islander seeking a separate cottage for children or grandchildren.

The story is told of a Chesapeake Bay islander who went to New York and, upon his return, was asked about that other great island he had visited, named Manhattan. "Well," he answered thoughtfully, "it'll never amount to much—it's too far away." Apocryphal or not, it is a story that could be told on Maine islands whose inhabitants treasure a worldview, neither right nor wrong, but different. This perspective includes a rather masochistic love affair with adversity, with the lack of conveniences (at least in comparison to life ashore), with the difficulty of transporting essentials from the mainland, with the necessity of walking—or biking—across island to get needed information. It is a worldview which finds satisfaction in a smaller scale and a less-frenzied pace of living in tune with the tides and the seasons. It is what helps make us a community.

F. Benjamin Carr

Glimpses

Fall

Vivid yellows and browns of rockweed and grasses along the shore

The sun setting below black rain clouds and turning the ledges on Goose and Sow and Pigs golden

Young eiders diving or running across the top of the water

Seas of invasive goldenrod turning from gold to fuzzy gray-brown

Our cove groaning beneath piles of eelgrass deposited by the high moon-tides

Tantalizing smells from home-built soups fit for royalty

Tent caterpillars settling into the puckerbrush for a long winter

Courtesy of Dean L. Lunt

The east side of Bustins Island.

A Maine Summer Island: The Story of Bustins

Courtesy of Dean L. Lunt

Typical island cottages with a view toward Chebeague.

Resplendent ferns, early spring bloomers, turn brown before the first frost

Flocks of Canada geese honking before daylight and feeding in the low-tide mud off Flying Point

Dark earlier in the evening and daybreak later in the morning

Charlie still back and forth, always when water is above mid-tide

Fall asters in varied shades of purple blooming in subdued splendor

Harvest moon rising over Goose like a round of ripe cheddar

Indian pipes, ghostly and pale, push up through the decaying oak leaves in clumps

F. Benjamin Carr

Jays thrashing noisily through the puckerbrush

Tomatoes finally, finally ripening just ahead of the first frost

Rose hips, red and succulent

Bumblebees blanketing the potted flowers on the deck

The seeds of touch-me-nots (jewelweed) explode at the touch

Concord grapes for the sampling on the arbor at Whitings—thank you, Norman!

Multicolored winter moorings, bright adornments to many yards while fresh paint dried, go overboard

Courtesy of Dean L. Lunt

Grandaughter Rachel bikes along the island's only road. There are no paved roads on Bustins.

A Maine Summer Island: The Story of Bustins

Courtesy of Linda Sweatt

Fall on Bustins south shore.

Smoke from the chimneys of the few cottages still in use

Huge dusty rose hydrangea blooms to be picked for dried floral arrangements before they turn brown

The Big Dipper with its handle seemingly close enough to grasp

Joan and Bob seaweeding their spectacular garden

Brilliant orange clusters of berries on the mountain ash below Garfield's The Ledges

Acorn road surface, as stable and comfortable as walking on rollerbearings, near As You Like It

Edible mushrooms pushing up at different spots on the golf course

Distant islands "loom" a mile high—an optical illusion of the season

F. Benjamin Carr

Flocks of scoters on the water

Squadrons of cormorants, wingtips nearly touching the water, fly single-file down the bay

Leftover green tomatoes appear at horsie-dervie time as late-season delicacies—fried greens

Columbus Weekend: boarding-up material leaning against sheds again, sad farewells

All docks and skiffs out but the Public as Alden awaits a full-moon, windless high tide

Frost scraped from the boat windshield

Water system drained, equipment serviced, rugs rolled up, storm doors on, gas off

Last trip ashore. Good-bye, Bustins; Hang in there, Lookout

Courtesy of Dean L. Lunt

The south side of Bustins looking past the Nubble toward Mere Point.

Epilogue

Time to Leave

TIME TO finish closing up the cottage. It is Sunday, the boat leaves at three o'clock this afternoon, and we need to be aboard. Another summer has sped by and now that time, so distant as to be out of mind at first glimpse of the island on Memorial Day Weekend, has arrived. We squeezed in a nostalgic last walk around the island yesterday. How long did it take? The timeless question asked for the final time this year elicits the classic, quick response, hallowed, true, and spoken whimsically: "It depends on whom you meet."

A number of people were about, most feverishly into their own idiosyncratic closing-up processes. They were glad for a moment's pause, glad for a final handshake, a hug, a "Stay in touch; we'll see you next summer."

We walked on. A few islanders, with relaxed superior airs about them, enjoyed the midday warmth of a quintessential fall day from the comfort of their porch rockers. They are the lucky ones without a deadline to meet—at least at the moment. They aren't leaving today. But their time will come.

The final hours are a hectic rat race of winterizing lawn-mower and generator motors, putting winter spars on moorings, stowing porch furniture, covering the garden with seaweed, draining the water system, making the cottage look as unappealing as possible to anyone who might look through the windows over the next months, dealing with anything from wine to V8 juice that might freeze, getting suitcases onto the lawn along with all the other odd-shaped boxes full of "stuff" going home to be repaired or discarded, waiting for the island truck to lug it down to the public float. Windows and doors exposed to the force of winter winds and snows are shuttered, and the knobs on the propane tanks are screwed down tightly to stop any flow of gas.

Finally, with the cottage battened down against winter's ravages, we rush to catch the boat that without fail, will cast off its lines at least a half-hour before we are really ready. Breathless, sweaty, dirty, collapsed on a bench, we peer across piles of luggage at other equally exhausted islanders. Then the questions begin to nag: Did I finally turn off those gas tanks? Did I padlock the little shed? We hardly have energy for a backward glance as Bustins recedes, or to find humorous the fatigue written over every face. Later as we drive the long miles and dusk approaches, I keep wondering what else I may have forgotten. And I chuckle, as I always do, at my brilliant and creative solution for avoiding all the stresses we have just undergone over the last couple days: Leave a week earlier!

Courtesy of Dean L. Lunt

Ben and Marilyn Carr, 2007.

F. Benjamin Carr

Courtesy of Dean L. Lunt

Ben and Marilyn Carr's Lookout as seen from the water.

One of the joys of Bustins is that we can go back again. We count down the months of the new year as Bustins-time draws closer. And then we are aboard the ferry once again, eagerly anticipating that moment after she rounds Wolfe's Neck, avoiding the ledges near Pound of Tea, when our straining eyes catch the first glimpse of Bustins ahead. We can cast our anxieties to the wind as the water, split by the ferry's bow, hisses by and our island, dressed in its soft spring colors, awaits our arrival. For all the ways the mainland encroaches, Turtle Rock still looms large and unchanged, reassuring us as we approach the Public. In our imaginations we can already hear the "cheeping" of ospreys overhead, the raucous crows caucusing in the oaks, the haunting call of the owl in the predawn dark, the scolding "chitter" of a red squirrel overhead on a dead stub. Soon we will exchange our watches for the ebb and flow of the tides, and immerse ourselves in the fullness of each moment. We will reunite with those life friends we have been longing to see, those gray-haired oldsters like ourselves with whom as teenagers we scavenged the shores for wooden pot buoys and danced through long summer nights. We will await the arrival in a month or so of children and grandchildren on whom, we sense, the island is imprinted just as it is on us.

Time passes. Life is moving on. The inevitability of change is, ironically, an unchanging verity of life. Over the last three decades of the twentieth century the mainland, with its agencies and rules, has encroached on our island to create a profusion of ties and obligations, many of them positive. But the island can no longer exist as it did for generations. If Bustins folk remember when "town and state pretended we didn't exist, and we pretended that they didn't exist," that time is no more.

For all this we know that new tales will emerge from our shared Bustins lives. They will be at once continuations of the old as well as brand-new tales springing from new happenings, evolving friendships, the changes brought by an encroaching main. If, as has been claimed, a myth describes something "that never happened but is always true," then these new tales will take their place in our island mythology, "the way things never were [perhaps] but always are." Their significance depends finally not on their factuality, but on what they tell us about our island and about ourselves, the secrets of who we are and the mystery of where our lives should go. They will touch our hearts and open our hearts. They will become pieces of an ongoing story that is always new, always fresh, always true. They are special gifts. For our island and for them—and for one another—we are deeply grateful.

About the Author

F. Benjamin Carr

Ben Carr's childhood home was Worcester, Massachusetts. He graduated from Worcester Academy and Cornell University and holds graduate degrees from Union Theological Seminary, Andover Newton Theological School, and the University of London. He and his wife Marilyn had been summer residents of Bustins Island for many years before they moved to Maine full-time in the early 1970s. Ben was a high school principal for twenty-one years at Narraguagus, Noble, and Southern Aroostook. When Marilyn was hired by the Machias School District in the late 1970s, she became the first public school art teacher in Washington County. She later taught art for many years at Massabesic Junior High School in Waterboro.

Combined, Ben and Marilyn have five children and seventeen grandchildren. When they are not on Bustins Island, they divide their time between Hancock, Maine, and the Caribbean island of Nevis.

Courtesy of Dean L. Lunt
Ben Carr, 2007.